THE SUPERIOR PERSON'S
BOOK OF WORDS

THE SUPERIOR PERSON'S
BOOK OF WORDS

PETER BOWLER

BLOOMSBURY

TO ASTRID

Be warned in time, James, and remain,
as I do, incomprehensible: to be great
is to be misunderstood.
— OSCAR WILDE

First published in Great Britain 2002

First US edition published in 1985 by
David R. Godine, Publisher, Inc.
Post Office Box 450, Jaffrey, New Hampshire 03452

Published by arrangement with David R. Godine Publisher Inc.,
9 Hamilton Place, Boston, Massachusetts 02108.

Bloomsbury Publishing Plc, 38 Soho Square, London W1D 3HB

A CIP catalogue record is available from the British Library

ISBN 0 7475 5337 8

Designed by Nathan Burton
Typeset by Dorchester Typesetting
Printed by Clays Ltd, St Ives plc

Acknowledgments

My sources are, naturally, impeccable (q.v.). They are far
too numerous to list in full, but I must acknowledge my
major, my most-often-referred-to, and in cases of doubts
my ultimate authority – the Australasian edition of
*Webster's New International Dictionary of the English
Language* (Merriam, Springfield and Sydney, 1912),
which has not only 2,662 pages and all the dirty words
but also a colored supplement of the flags of the world.
(Note: for the American edition of this book, we have
depended on *The American Heritage Dictionary*. – *Ed.*)

More importantly, I cannot let these definitions go
before the public without acknowledging the contribution
made by Dr. Ernest Foot, of The Chambers, Cheltenham,
who worked with me on the manuscript and wrote several
of the definitions. To me should go much of the credit for
whatever virtues this book possesses; the odium for any
faults must rest entirely with him.

Prolegomena

Words are not only tools; they are also weapons. The first object of this book is to provide the ordinary man in the street with new and better verbal weapons – words which until now have been available only to philologists, lexicographers, and art critics. Hitherto, the man who has known the precise meaning of *egregious, pejorative, exigent, pusillanimous* and *usufruct* has been able to enjoy a position of unfair advantage over the rest of us. We yield to him in debate, not because his arguments are more cogent, but because they are less intelligible. We accept him as a Superior Person because his vocabulary is a badge of rank as compelling as a top hat or a painted forehead.

Society may confine the ownership of top hats or painted foreheads to a favored few; but words are free, and available to all who aspire to them. There is nothing to prevent the butcher, the baker, or the candlestick maker from larding his speech with as many *pejoratives* as the Professor of English. All that is required is the simple effort of learning a mere hundred or so of those impressive words that lie just beyond the boundary of the average person's vocabulary – words that all of us have occasionally seen or heard without ever being quite sure exactly what they mean. And very little extra effort is needed to learn a further hundred or so words that are even less familiar – in some cases, virtually unheard of, but genuine and usable words nonetheless.

Five hundred such words are now brought together in this book. Learn them; use them; and by their use you may become a Superior Person.

Of course, there have been other books devoted to the listing and explaining of hard words. But this book goes beyond that. It offers, for the first time, practical guidance on how best to use these words in real-life situations. Thus the reader will learn not only the meaning of *aprosexia* but also how best to use it when filling in his sick-leave application form. Sample sentences are given for many words, showing how they can be used to confuse, deter, embarrass, humiliate, puzzle, deceive, disconcert, alarm, insult, intrigue, or even compliment – and all with relative impunity. Incoherent rage need no longer be the reader's only response when offended in public by an errant motorist, a noisy juvenile, or a *noisome alliaphage*; instead he will be able to smile sweetly and inform the offender that he or she is a *rebarbative oligophreniac* who deserves a *vapulation*. This is the Insult Concealed, of which there are many examples in this book – as there are of the Insult Apparent, the Compliment Questionable, and the Suggestion Surreptitious, as well as all sorts of other ways of using unusual words to gain one's ends, whatever they may be.

But if words are weapons, they are also toys. They are fun to play with. And here the author confesses to having indulged himself somewhat. Several of the words appearing in this book do so simply because he could not resist the temptation to revive a pleasing archaism or to reveal some little bizarrerie that had caught his fancy.

Pronunciations are not given, except for a very few special cases where the nature of the word positively requires it. The reader who genuinely wishes to equip himself with the vocabulary of a Superior Person should be prepared to submit to the intellectual discipline of finding out the pronunciations for himself.

Finally, a special message for any lexicographers or philologists into whose hands this book falls: the author may or may not have incorporated into the text, as a stimulus and a challenge to your perspicacity, one or more deliberate errors.

A

ABECEDARIAN *a.* (i) Arranged in alphabetical order; (ii) elementary, devoid of sophistication. The present book may be considered by some to fit both applications. For a more interesting meaning, see *unbeliever's defense, the.*

ABECEDARIAN INSULT, AN 'Sir, you are an apogenous, bovaristic, coprolalial, dasypygal, excerebrose, facinorous, gnathonic, hircine, ithyphallic, jumentous, kyphotic, labrose, mephitic, napiform, oligophrenial, papuliferous, quisquilian, rebarbative, saponaceous, thersitical, unguinous, ventripotent, wlatsome, xylocephalous, yirning zoophyte.' Translation: 'Sir, you are an impotent, conceited, obscene, hairy-buttocked, brainless, wicked, toadying, goatish, indecent, stable-smelling, hunchbacked, thick-lipped, stinking, turnip-shaped, feeble-minded, pimply, trashy, repellent, smarmy, foul-mouthed, greasy, gluttonous, loathsome, wooden-headed, whining, extremely low form of animal life.'

ABNEGATE *v.* Deny oneself. Not in itself a word of great usefulness. Included in this book because it is vital that the Superior Person not allow himself to be confused by the similarity between it and *abrogate* (repeal), *derogate* (detract), *abdicate* (renounce), and *arrogate* (claim). Note in particular that *abrogate* is not, despite appearances, the antonym of *arrogate*. The use of these words is advisable only for pipe-smokers, whose mid-sentence inhalations may afford sufficient time for the mental gymnastics necessary to ensure that the proper term is selected. Also recommended for pipe-smokers is *antimony* (q.v.).

ACEREBRAL *a.* Without a brain. A word for which there would at first sight appear to be no use, since no entity to which there would be any point in applying the term could in fact possess this attribute. (There would be no point in speaking of an acerebral windowsill.) However, recent researches into the central nervous system of the wire-haired terrier have conclusively demonstrated the need for such a word.

ADULATION *n.* Extravagant praise. An interesting example of a word whose usage is largely confined to the noun form, even though the verb form is readily available. Thus it would seem only natural for the author of this work to receive, on its publication, the adulation of an admiring public; whereas the notion of his being adulated by the public somehow conjures up a picture of his being submitted to some kind of indelicate physical process.

ADVISEDLY *adv.* Deliberately, with conscious intent (of words or phrases so used). Odd that it should have this meaning, since words used advisedly are almost invariably used not on the basis of the advice of others but on the basis of one's own convictions.

AEAEAE *a.* Magic. As in *aeaeae artes*, the magic arts. The only all-vowel six-letter word known to the author. The derivation is from Aeaeae, which was a surname of the legendary pig-fancier Circe and the name of a small island off the coast of Italy, said to have been her place of abode. Useful for unscrupulous players of parlor word-games. If taken to task for using it in such circumstances, you say: 'Well, yes, strictly speaking it is foreign, I suppose – at least in origin – but, surely, it's a word everyone *knows*, isn't it?'

AFFLATUS *n.* A sudden rush of divine or poetic inspiration. From the Latin *afflare* – to breathe or blow on. *Inspiration* itself means a breathing in. Why the ancients should have chosen the breath of the gods or muses – rather than their touch, voice, etc. – as the means of communicating super-human knowledge or creativity is not quite clear. While dining out with your beloved, you might suddenly put down your knife and fork, gasp, strike your forehead with your hand, lean forward tensely, and say, in unconcealed agitation: 'Jennifer, I think I've just had an afflatus!'

ALGORITHM *n.* A mathematical term derived from the name of an Arabian mathematician. Its usefulness to the Superior Person derives from its very obscurity of meaning, which permits it to be used safely in almost any context – a figure of speech, a bodily function, a musical notation, etc.

ALLIACEOUS *a.* Smelling or tasting of garlic or onion. From the bulb allium (*allium sativum,* garlic; *allium cepa,* onion). Garlic was added to food in southern Europe in the Middle Ages for the specific purpose of suppressing the unpleasant flavor of meat, fish, or poultry which had gone bad in the course of its typically slow journey from supplier to consumer; in the present age, it is added to food by persons of cultivated habits for the purpose of suppressing, for reasons unknown to the author, the pleasant flavor of meat, fish, or poultry which has not gone bad. According to the British Pharmaceutical Codex for 1934, cases have been reported where the internal administration of garlic has proved fatal to children; and, from the same source (for those in search of the ultimate frisson), the author reports that poultices made from pulped garlic are stated to be useful in accessible tuberculous lesions.

ALLIAPHAGE *n.* A garlic-eater.

ALOPECIA *n.* Baldness. The Superior Person should always be alert to the potential value of medical terms when properly used in lay conversation (see also *contraindicated*). Thus: 'My husband's alopecia is very bad this morning, Mr. Purbright; I'm afraid I may not be able to get in to the office before about eleven o'clock.'

ALTERNATE *a.* Each succeeding the other in turn (said of two things). It should not be necessary to point out the difference from *alternative* (also said of two things, but meaning 'available as a different option'); but it is. A bookshop in the capital city of Australia had a sign prominently on display advertising a collection of books on 'alternate living.' The author approached the books with interest, assuming them to be variant editions of *Dr. Jekyll and Mr. Hyde*, but found them to be a curious assortment of manuals of primitive agriculture and tracts devoted to the advocacy of atavism.

AMIABLE *a.* Likeable – but note that the meaning goes a little beyond this, and covers also the feeling of affection or friendliness for others. An amiable person therefore is one who not only is easily liked by others but also is of a friendly disposition, with a natural fondness for others. It is in the latter sense, presumably, that the term is used by Gibbon when he refers to rape as 'that most amiable of human weaknesses.'

ANABIOSIS *n.* Revival after apparent death; reanimation after a coma so deep that all the vital signs have become imperceptible. As you read the morning paper and sip your *ante-jentacular* (q.v.) coffee, you call out to your firstborn: 'Roger, just pop into the bedroom for a moment, will you, and see if anabiosis has set in with your mother yet.'

ANAESTHETIC, ANALGESIC, ANODYNE *a.* There are real differences in meaning between the three. The first, like a Henry James novel, induces insensibility; the second, like a newly broached bottle of Glenfiddich, makes you feel no pain; and the third, like the welcoming arms of your beloved, removes the cares of the world from your shoulders. Simple-minded listeners can sometimes be successfully duped by the use of *anodyne* as a *spurious* (q.v.) technical term. 'It has nine transistors, four diodes, and six anodynes.'

ANATHEMA *n.* A person or thing abominated by, and hence anathema to, someone. Less often used now in its proper sense of a formal curse pronounced by an ecclesiastical authority in the process of excommunication or denunciation. Like *plethora* (q.v.) recommended for use by lispers, in whose speech the deliberate use of the sound *th* can, properly managed, create a satisfying disorientation in the mind of the listener. *Anathematic*: a pathological gathper.

ANGLICIZATION *n.* Converting into English. Formerly used principally in relation to form, custom, or character. Now that there are no benefits to be derived from anglicization in that sense, its use is confined largely to the linguistic meaning, i.e., the translating into English of names, titles, etc. Thus: 'This is the BBC. Tonight we will hear a performance of the Complaining Songs, by Gus Crusher, sung by Elizabeth Blackhead.'

ANTABUSE *n.* Not, as you might be forgiven for thinking, the molestation of the formicidae, but the instrument of a form of obliquity which, if less bizarre, would appear equally deserving of *obloquy* (q.v.) – namely, the redemption of alcoholics by the administration of a drug, with the above trade name, which associates the consumption of alcohol with the most unpleasant consequences.

ANTE-JENTACULAR *a.* Pre-breakfast (see *anabiosis*). Goes nicely with *post-prandial* (after dinner).

ANTIMONY *n.* A poisonous metal. So called, according to tradition, because of its use in a famous case of mass poisoning of monks in the fifteenth century by an alchemist named, rather delightfully, Basil Valentine. Hence, *anti-moine*, or 'hostile to monks.' Its appropriate usage in the present century (i.e., the substance, not the word) would lie in its administration to people who smoke pipes in elevators.

ANTINOMY *n.* Contradiction between two authorities. Note that the accent is here on the second syllable instead of the first.

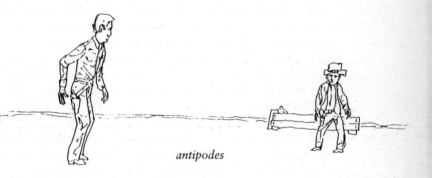

antipodes

ANTIPODES *n.* Diametrically opposite. The term has hitherto been used quite incorrectly to mean Australia. The author is glad of this opportunity to set the record straight by explaining that the antipodes are in fact the British Isles – a place on the very underside of the earth where wiry little pale-faced men and large plump rubicund men hang upside-down, wearing cloth caps and bowler hats res-pectively. The preference for tight-fitting headgear derives from an obvious necessity.

APOPHTHEGM *n.* *Highfalutin* (q.v.) word for an epigram. Much preferred to the latter, but easier to write than to say, in view of the problems presented by the central *ph*. Although the standard authorities permit the word to be pronounced *ph*-less, such a pronunciation would be extremely *infra dig* for a Superior Person, and should be eschewed in favor of the full version. Practice it, preferably in front of a mirror with your mouth full of salted peanuts. Become proficient in a few key sentences, such as: 'Now, Herr Doktor, is it not time for you to give us one of your little apophthegms?'

APORIA *n.* Patently insincere professings, e.g., by a public speaker, of an inability to know how to begin, what to say, etc. This is a very high-class word indeed, and should be used only in conversation with Samuel Beckett or Patrick White. Anyone else will assume you are referring to an unpleasant form of skin disease.

APOSIOPESIS *n.* Breaking off in the middle of a story. A rhetorical device. (See *oxymoron*.)

APROSEXIA *n.* Inability to concentrate. *Not*, as might incautiously be assumed, après-sex activities. Useful when completing the 'nature of illness' section on your sick-leave application form.

ARCANE *a.* Secret, hidden. An excellent example of a Superior Word of the first order, i.e., one that is on the margin of recognition for most people, is known to many, but used by few. Suggestive of strange and wonderful mysteries and powerful knowledge. The arcane lore of the tarot cards, etc.

ARIGHT *adv.* Correctly. The Superior Person should be equipped with a modest range of archaisms. Their use, in moderation, will add character to his discourse, endear him to at least one elderly female relative, and go some way toward retrieving for him the forbearance of his ever-dwindling coterie of friends. Never say, 'If I hear you correctly ...'; say, 'If I read you aright ...' Also recommended are *goodly*, as in 'a goodly number'; *gramercy* (q.v.); *peradventure* (q.v.); and, '*sit you down*' instead of 'sit down.' The phrase '*sit you down*' should always be accompanied by an Expansive Gesture.

ASPIC *n.* (i) A meat jelly in which pieces of meat, poultry, egg, etc. are set, to be served as savories. (ii) A glistening, slightly sweet-tasting slime used by airline companies to coat pieces of pork fritz, chicken-and-devon roll, etc., before serving them to entrapped passengers under the name of a light snack, or cold collation. In the latter regard, it is of course *decollation* (q.v.) that is in order for the caterer concerned.

ASPIRATOR *n.* Instrument for drawing pus from abscesses. Its natural usage is in the contemplative remark, made at the quiet fireside after the children have gone to bed. 'You know, dear, I've been thinking that it would be a nice gesture if we gave your uncle an aspirator for Christmas.'

ATARAXIA *n.* Absolute calm and tranquility; imperturbability; complete freedom from anxiety or strain. The condition of a lexicographer on reaching the word *zythum*, which, appropriately enough, means a kind of malt beer. A *zythepsary* is a brewery.

ATAXY *n.* Disturbance of bodily functions, especially that of motion. The interest of this word lies largely in the fact that it is pronounced exactly the same as 'a taxi.' The serious lexicologist should have at his command as many as possible such words, which permit the quiet enjoyment of many a deliberate ambiguity, in friendly or unfriendly discourse.

AUTOCHTHON *n.* Original inhabitant. A highfalutin synonym for *aboriginal*. Incidentally, there is no such word as *aborigine*; but *aborigines* is an acceptable plural for *aboriginal*.

AUTO-DA-FÉ *n.* The burning of a heretic, under the Inquisition. Literally 'act of faith.' Originally the term applied to the ceremony accompanying the pronouncement of judgment by the ecclesiastical authorities, after which the victim was handed over to the secular authorities for actual ignition; but gradually the latter came to be referred to as the auto-da-fé itself. The plural, incidentally, is *autos-da-fé*. Now that the auto-da-fé has been replaced, as an instrument for maintaining the True Church, by the Catholic Radio and Television Bureau, the nearest thing to the former is probably the author's backyard barbecues. Here the author performs the act of immolation, and the act of faith is on the part of his guests.

AVIGATION *n.* Absolutely brilliant neologism for aerial navigation.

AVUNCULAR *a.* In the manner of an uncle. An interestingly ambiguous – indeed multiguous – word, since there is no fixed or universal pattern of behavior for uncles. An experimental canvassing of the author's acquaintances revealed a widespread assumption that avuncular behavior was benevolent, mildly paternal, gently jocular, mature and dignified. However, one respondent admitted to having an Uncle Morris who was twenty-three years old, wore a gold earring in his nose, played viola da gamba with an innovative rock group, and had recently been expelled from the Hare Krishna movement for tattooing indelicate mandalas on the soles of his feet.

B

BAKLAVA, BALACLAVA *n.* The justification for including these words in this book is to warn the reader against confusing them with each other. The former is an exceedingly rich and sweet pastry, made in layers interspersed with, and permeated by, honey; the latter is a tight-fitting woollen head-covering. Any attempt to use a baklava as a head-covering, or to eat a balaclava, could lead only to the most dispiriting consequences.

BARBERMONGER *n.* A term used by Shakespeare in *King Lear* and defined by Johnson as 'a fop decked out by his barber.' In these days of unisex hairdressing salons and individual hairstyles for men, some reader even crustier and more conservative than the author may wish to revive this old term as a last defense against the inroads of male coiffurism. Repeatedly characterizing your dashing young coworker – the one with the Antonio Special No. 2 – as a barbermonger may at least irritate him, if nothing else, especially in view of the rather *infra-dig* (for him) connotations of the word *barber.*

BARMECIDE *n.* Insincere benefactor; one who holds out illusory offers, or who promises but does not deliver. One degree worse than an Indian Giver, since the latter at least delivers the goods, even if he does expect to get them back again, with interest. The original Barmecide is to be found in *The Arabian Nights*. A member of a wealthy Persian family, he decided to amuse himself one night by inviting one Schacabac, a wretched, starving beggar, to a sumptuous meal. Barmecide's little jape consisted of presenting Schacabac with a succession of grandly served courses, amid all the trappings of luxury – ornate bowls and dishes, magnificent table-settings, and so on – the catch being that there was no actual food in any of the receptacles placed before the hapless guest. The story ends with Schacabac taking it all in good humor and being rewarded for good sportsmanship with a real meal. The unsavory Barmecide was dealt with appropriately by Fate: his family became so magnificent that they aroused the enmity of the Caliph, who imprisoned or executed them; and the name of Barmecide himself has become synonymous with deceit, illusion, hypocrisy, and the proffering of bounty only to withhold it until the profferer's terms are met.

BASTINADO *n.* A punishment, of oriental origin, in which the soles of the feet are beaten. The term is useful for waiters who wish to preserve their dignity in dealing with the female American tourist. When she palpates and rejects the third avocado you have offered her and in so doing casts hyperaudible aspersions upon your integrity, you smile imperturbably and say: 'Would Madam perhaps prefer the Bastinado?' Alternatively, you might invoke the *strappado* –

a torture inflicted by hoisting the victim by his tied hands and then dropping him so that his fall is cut short by the taut rope before he reaches the ground.

BATHYBIUS *n.* A gelatinous deposit, dredged up in mud from the lower depths of the ocean. At first thought to be organic, but now known not to be. If unlucky enough to take your bath *after* your younger brother, you could use this term to describe the ring of waste-matter left on the sides of the bath for you to scrape off.

BATTOLOGY *n.* The continual reiteration of the same words or phrases in speech or writing. A battologer is one who battologizes. One of those words whose lack of wider currency seems undeserved and puzzling in the light of its wide potential for application to television commercials, sales pitches by car and encyclopedia vendors, spouse's homilies, etc.

BAVARDAGE *n.* Foolish or empty chatter. Attracts the adjective *mere*, in contradistinction to words such as *balderdash* or *poppycock*, which attract the adjective *absolute*.

BEDIZEN *v.* To trick out; to decorate, ornament, or dress up with more ostentation than taste. When Lady Festering makes her ceremonial entry at the charity ball, wearing her Christmas Tree Dress, you whisper to your companion: 'I'm told she goes to a professional bedizener.'

BELESPRIT *n.* A finer spirit, an intellectually gifted person. The purchaser of this book. The plural is *beauxesprits*.

BELLIBONE *n.* Believe it or not, 'a woman excelling both in beauty and goodness' (Dr. Johnson's Dictionary). One of a few words that the author has taken the liberty of disinterring from the past (even Johnson refers to it as 'not in present use') because of their obvious potentialities in polite discourse.

belomancy

BELLWETHER *n.* A male sheep which leads the flock, with a bell tied around its neck. Hence, anyone who assumes a leading role or takes the initiative – more appropriately, among a group of less than dynamic or purposeful colleagues. As, for example, the president of a Parents and Citizens Association.

BELOMANCY *n.* Predicting the future by the use of arrows. The future of the then reigning British royalty was accurately foretold in this fashion at the Battle of Hastings.

16

BIGGIN *n.* A silver coffee pot with a separate container which holds the coffee as it is heated. Always make a point of asking your hostess at least once during the evening if she has a biggin.

BIODEGRADABLE *a.* Capable of being easily broken down by natural decomposition, and hence not causing permanent pollution of the environment. A technical term that has in recent years been taken up by nontechnical environmentalists as part of their cant. Environmentalists are people, such as the author's children, who believe that to throw a Popsicle stick out of the car window is to pollute the environment, in contrast to the author, who thinks that a Popsicle stick *inside* the car pollutes the environment.

BOONDOGGLE *v.* or *n.* To carry out valueless or extremely trivial work in order to convey the impression that one is busy. Work so carried out. A necessary technique for military circles, where the classic form is the day-long carrying around of a rubbish bin while the remainder of your platoon are out on maneuvers. On being questioned by an officer, a smart 'Rubbish detail, sir!' satisfies the inquirer.

BOWLER *n.* In cricket, one who, on blundering badly, gets another chance – in contradistinction to a batsman, who does not. Natural blunderers should therefore always be bowlers. *Slow bowler:* one who opens the bowling for an English cricket team. *Fast bowler:* one who bowls to an Australian opening batsman. It will at once be apparent from the preceding definitions that one man may be both a slow and a fast bowler at the same time. Do not allow this to puzzle you – the game has its own metaphysics as well as its ritual and its regalia. (See *fallacy*.)

BUCENTAUR *n.* State barge of Venice, formerly used during the annual ceremony of the Marriage of Venice with the Adriatic. This ceremony was intended to establish and maintain the true and perpetual dominion of Venice over the Adriatic, which in its turn was to be subject to Venice as a bride is to her husband. The male chauvinist piggery implicit in this is reaping its just deserts as the Adriatic comes closer and closer to submerging Venice once and for all; and the Fathers of the State are now understood to be searching for a suitable barge with which to obtain a divorce.

BULLY FOR YOU! Nicely derisory congratulative. Thus, *A*: 'We made the trip down in just three and a half hours, and I pride myself on the fact that I didn't once exceed the speed limit.' *B*: 'Bully for you!' (See also *stout fellow!*)

BUMBLEPUPPY *n.* A nice, old-fashioned word which, according to the Concise Oxford Dictionary, means a game played with a tennis ball slung to a post. In other words, it is a perfectly correct if somewhat archaic term for any or all of those modern, glossily packaged and energetically promoted games with carefully invented, vigorous, clean-cut names such as Dyna-ball or Pole-a-Play. The connotations in *bumblepuppy* of bumbling and puppydogs give it a suitably condescending flavor for use when you arrive at your physical-fitness-fanatic sister's home and find her bounding around the back yard with her disgustingly athletic husband. 'Ah,' you say, 'I don't believe I've had a game of bumblepuppy since I was in kindergarten. You've bought it for the kiddies, have you?'

BUNKUM *n.* Claptrap. Both words seem to have acquired in modern parlance the meaning of nonsense, or balderdash; but the original meaning of the former is much more specific, and ought, in the view of the author, to be revived, especially for the purposes of political journalism. *Bunkum* in the original sense is a showy but insincere political speech made for the purpose of impressing one's constituents. One might say, therefore, that it is any political speech. The original spelling was *Buncombe*, and the original bunkum was spoken by Felix Walker, a backwoodsman from Buncombe, North Carolina, who insisted on dragging out the debate on the Missouri Question in the Sixteenth Congress, on the grounds that the people of Buncombe expected a speech from him.

C

CACOPHEMISM *n.* The opposite of *euphemism*; a harsh or pejorative expression used in place of a milder one. *Quack* instead of *doctor*, for instance. A *euphemism* is generally no more than the triumph of squeamishness over reality: *little person* for *dwarf*, *senior citizen* for *old man*, *disturbed* for *crazy*, etc. It is characterized by a lack of humor. Cacophemisms, on the other hand, tend to reflect an attitude of rough-and-ready good humor toward the person or object in question: *egghead, grease monkey, quack*, etc. A further difference between the two 'isms' is that cacophemisms are more readily recognized for what they are; euphemisms tend to have acquired a wider currency in normal parlance and hence to be accepted more unthinkingly by the listener. On the other hand, cacophemisms are more likely to have second meanings of their own, and this in itself can lead to confusion. If an Australian given to cacophemisms were to speak of a frog in a bog, he might be speaking of a marsh-dwelling amphibian; but he might also be speaking of a Frenchman in a toilet. The Superior Person would avoid such an ambiguity (unless, of course, it were deliberately sought after) by speaking not of a frog in a bog but a wog in a bog. Cacophemisms are not, however, the natural vehicle for the Superior Person's thoughts; he much prefers *charientisms* (q.v.).

CADUCEUS *n.* Everyone knows what a cornucopia is, but who knows what the deuce a caduceus is? It is in fact an object as familiar as the cornucopia. It is the serpent-entwined rod traditionally carried by Hermes, regarded until recently as a symbol of commerce, and now regarded as a symbol of the medical profession. The reason for the apparent linking of commerce and the medical profession is not clear to the author. Hermes was the herald and messenger of the gods, and supposedly the caduceus enabled him both to fly and to lull to sleep the souls of the dead before carrying them to the underworld. It might thus in modern times be more appropriately the symbol of air transportation, or of late-night television talk shows. The nonmagical caduceus was carried in ancient times by envoys when they were suing for peace. This is said to reflect the fact that the two serpents twined around it are kissing, or that they have just been separated by the rod from their previous combat.

CADUCITY *n.* (i) The dropping or shedding of a disposable part of an animal or plant when its function has been performed and it is no longer needed; (ii) hence, fleetingness, perishableness, or impermanence; (iii) hence, senility, proximity to dissolution. 'Oh, all right then, Aunt Maud, I'll go to Sunday

School – but only out of respect for your caducity.'
In the first sense mentioned above – the dropping of
a disposable appendage – the term might apply to
the author's toothbrushes, or his *zori* (q.v.).

CALEFACIENT *a.* A medicinal agent producing a feeling
of warmth. 'Calefacient, anyone?' you inquire as you
pass around the cognac.

CANARD *n.* A fabricated anecdote or sensational report;
a phony yarn; a hoax. A word that is familiar
enough, no doubt, to most readers; but how many
know the derivation? It is, of course, the French
word for duck, and this particular application
springs from a hoax perpetrated on the public by
one Cornelissen, who spread it abroad that he had
killed one of twenty ducks and fed it to the other
nineteen, who ate it; then similarly fed one of the
nineteen to the remaining eighteen; and so on, until
there remained only one duck – which had thus
eaten nineteen other ducks. The story was widely
covered in the papers of the time.

CARAVANSERAI *n.* The Superior Person's word for a
motel. Strictly speaking, a Middle Eastern caravan
park, consisting of what Webster calls a 'large, rude
unfurnished building' surrounding an open courtyard.

CARBUNCLE *n.* The usage to be preferred is not the
common pre-penicillin-era meaning of a larger-than-
life abscess, but the even earlier one of a red, pre-
cious stone. As in Conan Doyle's *The Blue
Carbuncle*, in which Sherlock Holmes traces the
train of events which led to the Countess of Morcar's

famous blue carbuncle being found in the crop of a dead goose. But why, in that context, a *blue* carbuncle? How can a gem which is by definition red be blue? Can the great detective have been guilty of an appalling aberration? He refers to the stone in question as being 'remarkable in having every characteristic of the carbuncle, save that it is blue in shade, instead of ruby red' – but this is on a par with saying that a mountain has every characteristic of a mountain save that it is flat! It is perhaps significant that Holmes places the supposed carbuncle in his strongbox with a casual remark to the effect that he will drop a line to the Countess of Morcar to tell her of its whereabouts – *but he never does, and the Countess herself never appears in person to claim her possession.* These are deep waters indeed. Can the Countess's carbuncle really have been an abscess instead of a gem, and if so how did it find its way into a goose's crop? Perhaps there is, behind all this, an even deeper and more chilling mystery than the great detective was prepared to reveal even to the good Dr. Watson. Be that as it may, the potential of the word itself in modern parlance is obvious. 'Ah, Lady Marbles, when I see you in that dress I have a vision of you with a great carbuncle resting upon your bosom.'

CARDIALGIA *n.* Heartburn, i.e., mild indigestion. To the uninitiated, however, *cardialgia* sounds like a serious disorder of the heart; hence suitable for excuses, sympathy-seeking ploys, etc.

CHARIENTISM *n.* An elegantly veiled insult. One of the various worthy ends to which this book is a means.

CHIMERA *n.* An interesting example of a word whose metaphorical usage has gradually moved away from the original sense. The currently accepted meaning is a fanciful conception or scheme, an unreal ambition, or even a castle in the air. But the original meaning was an imaginary monster, an unjustified fear, a bogy. The original Chimera was a fire-breathing female monster with the head of a lion, the body of a goat, and the tail of a dragon. She was said to have laid waste a district in Asia Minor before being killed by Bellerophon. So when your hoped-for liaison with the flighty Esmeralda fails to take place, and she admits to you that your place in her affections has been taken by the *saponaceous* (q.v.) Nigel, you sigh and say to her: 'Ah, well ... to me, Esmeralda, you must always remain a chimera, I suppose.'

CHREMATOPHOBIA *n.* Fear of money. The rarest complaint known to man. Sufferers from this condition, rejoice! Help is now at hand! Send all your money to the author, in a plain wrapper, and you need never know fear again!

CICURATE *v.* To tame, or reclaim from a state of wildness. 'Belinda, I'm not having that young man of yours in the house until he's been thoroughly cicurated.'

CIRCUMFORANEOUS *a.* Wandering from house to house. A Mormon, a Jehovah's Witness, an Avon Lady, a hungry cat, or a teenager.

CLERICAL *a.* (i) Of clergy, (ii) of clerks. There are very few words with as perfectly balanced an alternativity of meaning. And yet note how readily the meaning becomes polarized once the word is set in the context of a sentence ('Putting on his clerical garb, he ...'), of another single word ('clerical error'), or even of a prefix ('anticlerical'). Consider the phrases 'clerical gentlemen' and 'clerical officer.' There is no doubt about the meaning of the adjective in each case, even though an officer and a gentleman are traditionally supposed in some quarters to be one and the same thing.

COCKLE *n.* A word with even more different meanings than *gammon* or *gudgeon*. Everyone knows about the shellfish, but you should be able to disorient your friends completely with one or more of the other meanings set out as follows:

· A mineral occurring in dark, long crystals.

· A grasslike plant with black seeds growing among grain.

· A shallow boat.

· A stove, kiln, or furnace.

· A wrinkle or ripple. (Also, used as a verb, to wrinkle or to cause to wrinkle.)

· Whimsical.

· A cut or ringlet.

· To wobble.

· The inmost depths (as in 'the cockles of my heart' – possibly derived from the 'wrinkle' sense of the term).

· Perhaps most bizarre of all is the phrase 'to cry cockles' – eighteenth-century slang for 'to be hanged,' apparently derived from the distinctive gurglings emitted during strangulation.

CODGER *n.* Mean old fellow. The typical phrase is 'old codger,' even though the notion of age is already present in the word itself. (See also *whippersnapper*.)

COMICONOMENCLATURIST *n.* A specialist in funny names. The serious collector of funny names accepts only those of real people, and abides by certain rules of the game, just as do those who shoot quail or those who fish for trout. Chinese names are not fair game, and no self-respecting comiconomenclaturist would include in his collection a Ho Hum, a T. Hee, or a Jim Shoo. An interesting sidelight of the comiconomenclaturist's pursuit is the realization that names cease to be funny as they become famous, or even familiar – consider the case of Dingle Foot, Preserved Fish, or Mollie Panter-Downes.

CONSTABLE *n.* Originally 'count of the stable'; now the Australian police force's equivalent of an army private. The recommended form of address when speaking to any Australian police officer who is wearing badges of senior rank. When speaking to a constable, the recommended form of address is *Superintendent.*

CONTRADISTINCTION *n.* Why say 'in contrast with' when you can say 'in contradistinction to'?

CONTRAINDICATED *a.* Inadvisable. A technical term from the realms of medical/pharmaceutical jargon. 'For the treatment of headache, amputation is contraindicated.' A word that is surprisingly useful in nonmedical discussion. 'I think, darling, a visit by your mother at this particular time is contraindicated.' Familiarity with its use is also essential to reduce the natural sense of inferiority besetting the lay person who finds himself in the company of two or more doctors at any one time, e.g., at polo matches, afghan hound meets, antique auctions, or vintage-car rallies.

contraindicated

CORUSCATE *v.* Sparkle, twinkle, flash, glitter. Used in particular with regard to flashes of wit or intellectual illumination. Thus, Taylor's 'He might have illuminated his times with the incessant coruscations of his genius.' *Coruscating* may be used to good effect in place of *rapierlike*, even though the sense is quite different, in the example given under *remarks, exasperating* (q.v.).

COUNTERPANE *n.* Coverlet for a bed, e.g., a quilt or bedspread. *Not* a window, or table-top of some kind. A nice, nineteenth-century word. People who had counterpanes on their beds used mucilage instead of glue, took portmanteaus with them when traveling, used gazogenes instead of soda syphons, wore plimsolls instead of sandshoes, and served their children's cereal in porringers instead of bowls. Oddly enough, the word is a distortion of *counterpoint*, one of the meanings of which was a stitched quilt, from the Latin *culcita puncta*, or pricked mattress or cushion.

COXCOMB *n.* Conceited fool. Similar to *popinjay* (q.v.) in meaning, but with the emphasis perhaps more on the foolishness and less on the conceit, so the two terms can be used in the one vilification without redundancy. The derivation is from *cock's combe* – the cap originally worn by the professional jester, or fool. Faintly archaic maledictories of this kind are much to be preferred even to the more dramatic modern ones – especially when the person being denounced is younger than the speaker. (See also *whippersnapper*.)

CURMUDGEON *n.* Cantankerous codger. Both *curmudgeon* and *codger* apply to men only, and there appears to be no female equivalent. Perhaps *grimalkin*, an old she-cat or nasty old woman, comes closest to it; but it is not really synonymous.

D

DACTYLOGRAM *n.* Fingerprint. A casual reference to your having been invited by the authorities to let them have your dactylograms may give the listener the impression that you are a distinguished applied mathematician who is called in by the government from time to time in a consultative capacity.

DAFFODOWNDILLY *n.* The Superior Person's word for a daffodil.

DARK LANTERN *n.* A lantern with a shutter device enabling its light to be hidden. This apparently oxymoronic term must have puzzled many a twentieth-century reader of nineteenth-century fiction. The modern flashlight is, in effect, a dark lantern, the switch replacing the shutter.

DECALCOMANIA *n.* A transfer – i.e., a picture or design of some kind imprinted on a paper in such a way as to permit its being transferred, after wetting, to another surface. Nowadays what used to be called simply *transfers* are coming to be called *decals* – which is simply an abbreviation of the above word. The Superior Person will always use the full word (the *c*'s are hard and the stress is on the 'cal'): 'I like your son's room, Mrs. Afterbath, but I was rather staggered by his decalcomania.'

DECANAL *a.* Pertaining to a dean. Originally an ecclesiastical term, but there is no reason why it should not find currency in the groves of academe. Thus, when the Dean of Intercultural Studies observes a student sit-in team approaching his office, the sedative for which he reaches might be referred to as the decanal seconal.

DECOCTION *n.* The Superior word for soup. Actually, anything prepared by boiling something in water to extract its essence. Note that soup can also be a concoction – provided it contains more than one ingredient, since a concoction is something prepared by cooking things in combination, or by combining things for some other purpose. This book is a concoction.

DECOLLATION *n.* Decapitation, beheading. See also *defenestration* and *jugulation*. 'And finally, ladies and gentlemen, girls and boys, I cannot let this speech night come to an end without a special mention for our Assistant Principal. We all know just how much he has contributed to the school over many years and what he means to us all – and I know you'll agree with me that, for everything he has done, for being what he is, he fully deserves a thoroughgoing decollation.'

DECORTICATE *v.* To strip or otherwise remove the bark, or husk, from; in other words, to peel. 'Would you care to decorticate a grape for me, O my beloved?'

DEFENESTRATION *n.* The act of throwing someone or something out of a window. A word that is neologism's paradigm and justification. If the word were not needed to describe the act, the act would need to be performed to justify the word.

DEFICIT FINANCING *n.* A method of disproving the Micawber theory of budgetary financing, by achieving an annual expenditure higher than annual income. The technique seems to be restricted, for no apparent reason, to national governments.

DESUETUDE *n.* State of disuse. Some nouns have their inevitably accompanying adjectives ('ineffable bore,' etc.); *desuetude* has its inevitably accompanying verb – 'fall into.' Desuetude is never arrived at, achieved, experienced, or enjoyed; it is invariably fallen into. How nice to be able to say to your visiting sister Agatha, when she makes her ritual inquiry into the piano-playing of your ten-year-old son, Roger, that it has recently fallen into desuetude. It is possible that she will assume you to be referring to an especially difficult piece by Chopin that the lad is now learning.

DETERRATION *n.* Not the act of deterring, but the discovery of an underlying object by the removal of the earth surrounding it. From the Latin *de* and *terra*. 'Young man, you will proceed immediately to the bathroom. The time has come for the deterration of your feet.'

DIGNITARY *n.* An important person occupying a high and exalted office. As, for instance, the Archbishop of Canterbury. (Cf. *luminary*.)

DIMISSORY *a.* Sending away; permitting to depart. In ecclesiastical usage, applied to the document conveying a bishop's authorization for a candidate for the ministry to be ordained somewhere else; the candidate is said to be given his dimissory letters. When midnight approaches and Brett and Margaret are *still* sitting there talking, you say to your helpmeet: 'Well, my dear, isn't it time we offered Brett and Margaret a dimissory coffee?' If Brett says brightly, 'What's that?' you explain: 'Oh, I suppose it's more or less the nonalcoholic equivalent of a doch-an-doris.' 'What on earth's a doch-an-doris?' asks Margaret. 'Oh,' says your helpmeet, 'it's more or less the same as a stirrup cup.' At this point both Brett and Margaret start making excuses to go. A doch-an-doris, or a stirrup cup, is a last drink – one for the road – offered to the departing guest more or less at the door.

DINGLE *n.* A narrow, wooded vale, dale, or dell. (Note that the last three words are synonyms for each other, and mean a small valley or ravine.) Incidentally, never confuse (unless you do so deliberately) the use of *tingle* with *tinkle*, as in the phrase 'to give someone a tinkle,' i.e., a ring on the telephone. (See also *umbriferous*.)

DIRHINOUS *a.* With paired nostrils. As, for example, the human face. Everyone is dirhinous, but few know it. A good word, therefore, for the Insult Apparent. 'Sir, you are a dirhinous mesomorph.' Similarly useful is *poriferous* (with pores) or *bimanal* (with two hands).

DIRIGIBLE *a.* Everyone is familiar with this word as a noun meaning airship; but of course it is originally an adjective meaning 'capable of being directed, steerable.' Thus an airship was a dirigible balloon. When the party is breaking up and everyone is starting to worry about Melanie, who is upright but distinctly glassy-eyed, you ask: 'Is she still dirigible?'

DISCALCEATE *a.* The Superior Person's word for *bare-footed*. From the Latin *calceus*, a shoe.

DISSIGHT *n.* Unsightly object; eyesore. 'Come in, old chap, come in! You're a dissight for sore eyes!'

DITTOGRAPHY *n.* and **HAPLOGRAPHY** *n.* Mistakes in printing or writing. In the former case, part of a word is repeated when it should appear only once; in the latter, part of a word appears only once when it should be repeated. A disadvantage of the author's neologism *unundulating* (q.v.) is that the reader, when confronted with it, may never be completely sure that is is not a dittography for *undulating* – or that *undulating* is not a haplography for *unundulating*.

DRAGOMAN *n.* Nothing to do with dragons, but an interpreter/guide; one who, in Middle Eastern countries, in the days when the Englishman's castle was never his home, insulated the visiting Old Etonian from the milling *autochthons* (q.v.) and insured that the former's jodhpur-filled portmanteaus reached more or less the same destinations as he did.

E

ECONOMICS *n.* An arcane language, used by its own cognoscenti for reviewing past events in the production and distribution of wealth. There are some who would define economics as a science rather than a language; but, in the absence of any evidence that future events can be predicted by economists on the basis of fixed laws, this approach can hardly be supported by the objective lexicographer.

ECTOMORPH, ENDOMORPH, MESOMORPH *n.* Psychology's contribution to the English language. The terms simply mean tall thin person, short fat person, and middle-sized person, respectively – but they look much more impressive than those more old-fashioned terms in a thesis on behaviorism or in an appallingly expensive textbook. They are, moreover, useful for insulting or alarming the ignorant: 'Sir, you are a miserable mesomorph'; 'One more remark like that about Mrs. Carr-Willoughby, my good man, and I shall see to it that the world knows of your ectomorphic tendencies.'

EFFENDI *n.* Turkish title used to show respect when addressing a government official. Try using it when next you call in at the IRS to plead your case; when explaining to the bus driver exactly how it was that you lost your ticket; when scrounging for school-project material for your daughter at the tourist bureau; or when registering your VW.

EFFLEURAGE *n.* A gentle stroking or caressing technique used in massage. In view of the suggestion of *fleur* and *corsage* embodied in this largely unfamiliar word, you might shyly ask your beloved to let you give her an effleurage before you go to the ball. You might even claim to be an advocate of multiculturalism and invent an old *ethnic* (q.v.) custom under which both partners give each other effleurages before going to the ball. And, for that matter, afterward as well.

EGREGIOUS *a.* Exceptional. An interesting example of a word that has gradually changed from complimentary to *pejorative* (q.v.) in its usage, being now most commonly found immediately preceding the word *ass*. Interestingly akin to *consummate* in the latter regard. In its Latin origin, it carries the sense of 'out of the herd' – cf. *gregarious*. It is an excellent word for insulting strangers with. 'Sir, you are an egregious rogue (ass, rascal, blunderer, etc.).' It sounds unpleasant, and it leaves the wretched object of your wrath uncertain as to just how insulting you have been. Even more effective in this way, though of course totally unjustified on lexical grounds, can be the use of the term on its own. 'Sir, you are egregious.' Needless to say, the term should be used thus only when you are quite certain that the person you are addressing is unaware of its meaning.

EMBONPOINT *n.* Plumpness. From the French *en bon point* (in good shape). Often used of women, and with just a trace of raillery implied. Commonly pronounced in the French fashion; but may be anglicized, in which event you would choose a moment when your neighbor, the *zaftig* (q.v.) Mrs. Frobisher, is displaying her new sewing machine to your wife, to tell her how much you admire her embonpoint.

EMUNCTORY *a.* or *n.* Of nose-blowing; an organ of the body that disposes of waste products. 'Our speaker tonight is well known to all of you. His emunctory achievements are an object lesson for all of us.'

EPHECTIC *a.* Habitually suspending judgment; given to skepticism. Like *aporia*, an exceptionally Superior word. The fact that ephecticism generally engenders ineffectualness should enable you to develop one or two phonically pleasing sentences. Alternatively, cultivate its use in the same sentence as *eclectic* (wide-ranging in acceptance of doctrines, opinions, etc.).

EPHEMERAL *a.* Short-lived, lasting but a day. Note that this does not mean trivial – a sense in which it is sometimes used. A devastating explosion is an ephemeral event.

EPICENE *a.* Androgynous; having both male and female characteristics; hermaphroditic. Derived from the Ancient Greek for 'on common ground' and originally used as a grammatical term signifying a noun whose form did not change whether for masculine or feminine gender. A secondary meaning which now seems to be in the process of taking over from the primary meaning is *weak, feeble,* or *effeminate.* It is worthy of remark that a word which means feeble is so similar in structure to *epicenter*, which means the ground above the center of an earthquake. If you wish to upbraid an androgyne, *epicene* is probably the term to be preferred, if only because of its phonic similarity to *obscene.*

EPONYMOUS *a.* Giving one's name to a book, an organization, etc. David Copperfield is the eponymous protagonist of *David Copperfield* – a fact which, if only it had been realized by Dickens at the time, might have effectively deterred him from writing the book. Not to be confused with *titular* (q.v.).

EQUANIMITY *n.* Calmness, unconcern. For maximum effect, use in a context where the reverse of this meaning is foreshadowed by the preceding words, e.g., 'I must admit, Arbuthnot, that the prospect of our losing you is one that we all face with no little equanimity.'

EQUITATION *n.* The art, or the act, of horse-riding. 'Has she shown any tendency to indulge in equitation?' you tactfully whisper to your sister as your pubescent niece leaves the room.

EREPTION *n.* Snatching away. Do not confuse with *ereptation* (creeping forth). Snuggling up to your beloved at the drive-in, you say, 'I think I sense an ereption coming on,' and suddenly snatch the M&Ms from her lap. If it transpires that she has put the M&Ms somewhere else, you will be compelled to perform an ereptation.

ERGASIOPHOBIA *n.* Fear of, or aversion to, work; diffidence about tackling the job. Another good word for using on sick-leave application forms.

ESURIENT *a.* Of a greedy disposition. The preferred usage is metaphorical, of a person's general character, rather than literal, of his eating habits. Rhymes rather nicely with *prurient* and *luxuriant*.

equitation

ETHNIC *a.* Pertaining to race, ethnological. *Not*, as so many seem to think, 'funny little foreign (person or thing),' as in ethnic radio, ethnic knits, or even ethnics.

ETHNOCENTRIC *a.* Firmly convinced that the characteristics of one's own race or culture are superior to those of any other. As, for example, those Australians who believe that Aboriginals should be taught to acquire the traditional culture and values of Western European civilization; or, for another example, those Aboriginals who believe that they should not.

41

ET HOC GENUS OMNE *phr.* And all that sort of thing. Why say *etc.* when you can say *et hoc genus omne*?

ETIOLATED *a.* Pale and drawn. A fin de siècle term, much encountered in the novels of George Moore. Since the listener can be safely assumed to be unfamiliar with its meaning, it may be used on any occasion at all ('My dear, you look positively etiolated'), the meaning being left to the imagination.

EUTHENICS *n.* The science of improving the condition of humans by improving their surroundings. In contradistinction to *environmentalism*, which is the science of improving the surroundings of humans by improving the humans. Likely to be confused in the listener's mind with *euthanasia*, enabling you to suggest, with perfect innocence, that your mother-in-law ought to be subjected to euthenics; on being questioned, you explain that you had in mind that she move into a modern home unit.

EVANESCENT *a.* Fleeting, vanishing, impermanent. When your wife's weekly number is the Grand Prize-winner in the lottery but you admit to her that you omitted to buy her ticket that week, her effervescence is evanescent.

EXIGENT *a.* Exacting, demanding, pressing. Thus *exigency* is a sudden requirement or pressure. Important to distinguish this from *exiguous*, which means meager or scanty. Thus, when one's lifestyle is exigent of resources, but one's resources are exiguous, one shortly becomes indigent.

EXPOSTULATE *v.* To reason earnestly. One of a group of words (*matriculate* is another) which can be used to some effect, in the right circumstances, as faintly suggestive of acts too indelicate to be referred to explicitly by the author of this book. 'There they were, expostulating under a tree,' etc. Useful for disconcerting Seventh Day Adventists.

EXUNGULATE *v.* To trim or cut the nails or hoofs. 'Mom, it really is too much! I wish you could do something about it; it makes me sick. Richard is in the bathroom, exungulating himself again.'

F

FABULIST *n.* An elegant euphemism for *liar.*

FACETIAE *n.* Facetious sayings. 'Greetings, Herr Doktor! Can I perhaps express the hope that you will tonight favor the assembled company with some of your little facetiae?'

FACINOROUS *a.* Exceedingly wicked. 'I will speak no ill of my opponent in this election campaign. All of us recognize and accept his truly facinorous nature.'

FALLACY *n.* Deluded belief. The three major fallacies of our time are that green does not go with blue, that wine tastes better than lemonade, and that the most effective type of bowler on a sticky wicket is a slow left-arm spinner.

FALL-BACK *a.* Less satisfactory, but acceptable as a last resort. As in 'fall-back position.' Negotiators typically go to negotiations equipped with Demands, Ultimate Objectives, Ulterior Motives, Acceptable

Compromises, and Fall-Back Positions. Not, however, the Superior Person. He is aware that there are, strictly speaking, only two possible fall-back positions – prone and supine.

FAMULUS *n.* A medieval sorcerer's assistant. A pleasing appellation for your husband when he is helping you in the kitchen by peeling the potatoes, drying the dishes, etc. – or when you are entertaining. 'Come into the living room and make yourself comfortable while I have my famulus mix some drinks.'

felicide

FANDANGLE *n.* (i) Silly fooling around; (ii) eccentric or grotesque ornament or ornamentation. 'Simon, this is Miss Finister, who is going to baby-sit for us tonight. Now I don't want you pestering the life out of her to look at your fandangle all the time, the way you did with poor Miss Parmenter.'

FELICIDE *n.* Killing a cat. 'Mom, do you think it's safe for Cicely to play with Rover? After all, he *is* felicidal.'

46

FIRKIN *n.* A small tub for butter. The author has nothing to say about this word other than to point out that the world awaits the poet who can successfully rhyme *firkin, gherkin,* and *merkin* (q.v.) in the one work.

FLAGELLATE *a.* Sending out long threadlike runners, as for example the strawberry. Suggestive, for obvious reasons, of *vapulation* (q.v.). 'Well, Brother Ambrose,' you say on your annual visit to the old school, 'still having as much fun as you used to with your flagellates?'

FLAGITIOUS *a.* Atrocious, heinous, appallingly wicked. Suggested for use where *facinorous* (q.v.) is not strong enough.

FLAPDOODLE *n.* Poppycock, balderdash. Three magnificent words of identical signification, i.e., rubbish, nonsense, empty and meaningless talk. The author much prefers the first, partly because it is the most ludicrous in sound, and partly because of its potential use in alliance with *fopdoodle* (q.v.).

FOLIE DE DOUTE *n.* Pathologically obsessive doubt about anything and everything done by the sufferer. At once the most touching and the most charming of neuroses. To quote from *Anomalies and Curiosities of Medicine*, by G. M. Gould and W. L. Pyle (1896): 'Gray mentions a case in a patient who would go out of a door, close it, and then come back, uncertain as to whether he had closed it, close it again, go off a little way, again feel uncertain as to whether he had closed it properly, go back again, and so on for many times. Hammond relates the history of a case in an intelligent man who in undressing for bed would spend an hour or two determining whether he should first take off his coat or his shoes. In the morning he would sit for an hour with his stockings in his hands unable to determine which he should put on first.'

FOPDOODLE *n.* An insignificant fool. From *fop* and *doodle* (the latter meaning, in this context, a trifler or idler). Not dissimilar to *popinjay* and *coxcomb*. The author prefers *fopdoodle*, for reasons similar to those given in the definition of *flapdoodle* (q.v.).

FORMICATE *v.* To swarm like ants. 'Principal, I thought you ought to know – the Seventh Grade is formicating all over the quadrangle.'

FRAMBOESIA *n.* A contagious tropical disease, with yellowish or reddish swellings resembling raspberries or strawberries, on the face, genitals, etc. A word of obvious utility for cursing and ill-wishing. The invoking of visitations by bizarre diseases, or by common diseases portentously named, upon those who offend you is an art in itself. Other useful words in this context are *murrain* (infectious cattle disease – metaphorically, a synonym for *plague*), *pellagra* (skin deterioration, diarrhea, and mental decay), *alopecia* (q.v.), *seborrhoea* (dandruff), *quinsy* (an abscess on the tonsil), *rhinorrhoea* (runny nose), *acariasis* (infestation by mites), *parotitis* (mumps), *rinderpest* (cattle-plague), and *malanders* (a scabby eruption behind the knee in horses).

FUGLEMAN *n.* A drill-sergeant or other soldier who stands in front of a group of drilling soldiers so that they can follow his lead; hence, any front-man, spokesman or leader who cuts an imposing figure and compels the members of an organization to dance to his tune. For example, the president of your local school's Ladies' Auxiliary Group – or would this be a *fugleperson*?

FULSOME *a.* Excessive; cloying through surfeit. As, for example, the praise given by a British sports commentator to the performance of the British swimmer who has just come last in the first heat of his event in the Commonwealth Games. Derived from *full*, but applicable only, oddly enough, to praise. One does not speak of fulsome criticism, or of fulsome abuse.

FUNGIBLE *a.* Replaceable by, or acceptable as a replacement for, a similar item. A legal term pertaining to goods supplied under contract. From the Latin *fungi* (*vice*) – to do (in place of). Your sister's latest boyfriend could be referred to as 'one of Belinda's fungibles.'

FUSTIAN *n.* or *a.* Ridiculously pompous, bombastic, or inflated language. The essence of fustian is not the use of big or exotic words but the adoption of a declamatory style that is unsuited, by virtue of its high-flown and flowery imagery, or its grandiose delivery, to the purposes for which it is being employed. Thus, any actor's speech delivered at any Oscar presentation ceremony; any address to a public gathering by any union official; any television commercial for any car or laundry detergent; any tourist guide describing any tourist attraction.

FUTTOCK *n.* A particular wooden component – the exact nature of which is unknown to the author – in the structure of a ship. A ridiculous word. If you have a yachting or otherwise nautical friend, make a point of always greeting him with the cheerful inquiry: 'And how are your futtocks these days, old bean?'

FYLFOT *n.* Swastika. 'Hoist the fylfot, your father's here!' you cry out to the children as your husband enters the room during one of his more dictatorial moods.

G

GALACTOPHAGOUS *a.* Milk-drinking. *Galactophage* could serve as a synonym for *milksop*. 'Now listen, you sniveling galactophage ...'

GALLIGASKINS *n.* Trousers, pants, breeches. Originally, loose-fitting wide hose or breeches of the sixteenth and seventeenth centuries, supposedly of Gascon origin. Suitable appellation for your wife's pantyhose, your daughter's *equitation* (q.v.) costume, or your golfing partner's expensively tailored tweed casuals.

GALOOT *n.* Loutish, clumsy oaf. *Oaf*, incidentally, comes from the same root as *elf* and originally meant an elf-child, a changeling – hence a simpleton or idiot. Galoots, however, are more clumsy than stupid; and there is a suggestion of likability in the term, the impression it conveys being that of a well-meaning but dimwitted show-off who overreaches himself. Use it by itself, without its usual companion *clumsy*, to bring out to the full its rather special charm.

GAMMON *n.* Of interest because it is one of those odd words that have multiple meanings, some of which have no obvious relation to each other. (See also *gudgeon*.) *Gammon* can mean:

· A leg or thigh.

· Smoked piece of bacon.

· To talk misleadingly and deceitfully (thus, you could gammon the lady behind the delicatessen counter by telling her how much you admire her gammon).

· The words used when gammoning, in the latter sense.

· The game of backgammon.

· A particular way to win at backgammon.

· To fasten a ship's bowsprit to the stem.

GARB *n.* Attire. A ridiculous word. Derived, believe it or not, from the Italian *garbo*, meaning elegance. Etymologically quite unrelated to *garbage* or *garble*.

GELOGENIC *a.* Laughter-provoking. As you line up the assembled family to be photographed on the occasion of their Christmas reunion, you look through the viewfinder and exclaim: 'Ah, good, good … Jennifer, would you mind standing slightly in front of Arthur? You're a little more gelogenic, I think.'

GENEALOGY *n.* The tracing of descent from ancestors; alternatively, a particular account of such a tracing for a specific individual or family. In the English-speaking world, all those who take up this pursuit announce sooner or later that they can trace their descent back to Edward III. This should surprise no one with a rudimentary knowledge of mathematics; there are probably one or two well-bred basset hounds who could also trace their descent back to Edward III. What is really surprising is that Edward III seems to be regarded as some kind of ultimate antecedent beyond whom the genealogist does not venture, even though anyone descended from Edward III is also descended from his father Edward II, and so on. The author can guess only that the prudery of the late Victorian age (when genealogy became a family pastime) chose to draw a veil before the memory of Edward II in view of the sybaritic Plantagenet's bisexual reputation and appalling death (see *impalement*).

GENIAL, GENUAL *a.* *Genial* (pronounced geenial) means warm, cheering, sociable; but it originally meant nuptial, or to do with generation – the genial bed was the nuptial bed. *Genial* (pronounced gennial), however, means pertaining to the chin, and *genual* means pertaining to the knee. Casual references to your genial (pronounced gennial) or genual organs can be quite effective in an appropriate context.

GERONTOCRACY *n.* Government by old men. As, for example, the administration of amateur athletics, tennis, swimming, etc.

GLABROUS *a.* Having a surface free from hair or other projections. Smooth-skinned, smooth-leafed. When introducing a guest speaker who suffers from alopecia (q.v.), you could insert into your remarks a passing reference to his 'glabrous pinnacle' without giving offense.

GNOME *n.* A word whose special interest lies in its secondary sense of aphorism, maxim, or pithy saying. Thus *gnomic* means either consisting of aphorisms, having the quality of an aphorism, or given to the use of aphorisms. When your sententious employer, a man of less than average height, returns from his holidays and greets you with a particularly pithy remark, you say brightly: 'Ah, you're just as gnomic as ever, I see, Mr. Bolingbroke!'

GNOSIS *n.* Knowledge of spiritual truth and of the deeper wisdom that is concealed from those without the necessary faith or insight. As claimed by the Gnostics. An ecclesiastical *dignitary* (q.v.) who finds himself on a television talk show, defending the faith against the earnest protestations of a pair of agnostics, could suddenly lean forward, as though he had just noticed something, and say, urgently but in a low voice: 'For heaven's sake! Whatever's happened to your gnosis?' His adversaries will spend the rest of the program rubbing their faces with studied nonchalance and worrying about their appearance.

GODWIT *n.* A marsh-wading bird with a long, upward-curving bill. One can only wonder at the derivation; but the potential of the term for the denigration of the sanctimonious is obvious.

GONGOOZLER *n.* One who stares for hours at anything out of the ordinary (such as the word *gongoozler*).

GOSSOON *n.* Lad. From the French *garçon*. Conveys a suggestion of ludicrousness, no doubt because of the listener's subconscious awareness of other words that end in *-oon*, such as *goon* and *loon*. Suitable therefore for use by an adult wishing to address a young male person – particularly a waiter – patronizingly.

GRACILE *a.* Slender. Not connected etymologically with *graceful*, but the obvious similarity in spelling inevitably has its effect on the impression conveyed, which is thus one of 'gracefully slender.' A beautiful word meriting revivification.

GRALLATORIAL *a.* Pertaining to long-legged wading birds. From the Latin *grallator*, or stilt-walker. A dignified way to describe the gait of your lankier acquaintances.

GRALLOCH *v.* To disembowel a deer. From the Gaelic word for intestines. The existence of the term implies the prevalence of the act, which the author assumes to be one of the pastimes of the English upper classes, along with fox-chasing, train-spotting, and bird-murdering.

GRAMERCY *int.* The Superior Person's way of saying thank you. A graceful archaism well worth reviving. From *grand merci*. Can also be used as an exclamation of surprise, meaning, more or less, 'mercy me!' Equally delightful in this sense. The ideal use is on occasions which inspire both surprise and gratitude, as for instance when there is a sudden power blackout just as your sister has put on one of her Scott Joplin records.

GRAMPUS *n.* A blowing, spouting, whalelike sea-creature with a blunt head and having teeth only in the lower jaw. The heavy-breathing fat person who sits beside you in the bus. A plausible nickname for Grandfather.

GRANDILOQUISM *n.* A grandiloquent utterance or term; a grandiose expression used in place of a more common one, just as a euphemism is a mild or delicate expression used in place of a blunt one; any word in this book – including, now that you mention it, the word *grandiloquism*.

GREGORY-POWDER *n.* A laxative powder, containing rhubarb, magnesium, and ginger, invented by a Scottish doctor named Gregory, who died in 1822, which should surprise no one. 'Mmmm,' you murmur appreciatively as you try the herbal powder your hostess has just sprinkled on your spaghetti Bolognese, 'it's not unlike gregory-powder, isn't it?' Without noticing your triple negative, she agrees happily.

GRIDE *v.* To scratch, scrape, or cut with a sound that grates upon the ears. An expressive and useful word that deserves to be better known and more often used, especially in relation to the drawing of a finger across a blackboard, or the compositions of serious musicians of the present day.

GROAK *n.* One who stands around while others eat, in the hope that he will be invited to join in. A good name for a female relative's boyfriend. 'How's your galactophagous groak these days, young Jennifer?' you inquire patronizingly.

GROYNE *n.* This is the correct term for one of those little wooden fences or brick walls that run down English beaches and out into the water for some distance, as a device to check the drifting of the same. Pronounced, and sometimes spelled, *groin*. 'Shall we get together down by the groyne?'

gride

GUDGEON *n.* One of those rather delightful words that sound as though they can, and in fact do, mean practically anything. A gudgeon can be:

· A pivot at the end of a rod, serving as the base for a rocker or wheel.

· A ring that fits over a hook to keep a gate closed.

· A pin connecting two blocks of stone.

· A pin holding a piston rod and a connecting rod together.

· A metal eye or socket on the stern of a boat, to receive the rudder.

· A gullible person.

· A bait.

GULOSITY *n.* Gluttony. (See also *guttle*.) It is astonishing just how many now-obsolete words refer to over-eating; presumably this reflects the social mores of bygone days. There are indications of a returning need for a range of terms of this kind, and the Superior Person would be well-advised to equip himself with some of the more esoteric.

GUMMA *n.* Syphilitic tumor. The plural is *gummata*. 'Where's Uncle Andrew now, for God's sake?' you can safely exclaim in the presence of the children. 'In the bedroom again, playing with his gummata?'

GUTTLE *v.* To eat gluttonously; to gourmandize; to show *gulosity* (q.v.).

GYNAECEUM *n.* Women's apartments in an ancient Greek or Roman house or other building. A nicely high-flown, whilst slightly deprecatory, way to refer to your sister's bedroom.

H

HA-HA *n.* A boundary to a park or garden, usually in the form of a fence sunk in a ditch. The nature of the term evidently derives from the consideration that a fence without a ditch, or a ditch without a fence, might ordinarily serve the purpose of a boundary, but a fence *in* a ditch would appear to be broadly comparable, in terms of actual usefulness, with a tower in a well.

HALIDOM *n.* Some readers will be familiar with this archaism through its use in the expression 'by my halidom'; but few will be aware that its meaning is 'holy thing,' so that the expression just mentioned really means 'by my holy thing.' You may care to cultivate the use of the translated version.

HAMADRYAD *n.* One of those rather delightful words that have several totally different meanings. A hamadryad can be a tree-dwelling nymph, a venomous Indian snake, or an Abyssinian baboon. You may thus use the word, for example in the latter sense, when insulting a female, but on being taken to task you may if you wish explain that you were using the word in its nymphal sense. Alternatively, you may use the word as an apparent compliment, conveying by your manner the impression that you are invoking the nymphal sense, but at the same time revel in the private knowledge that one of the other senses is the applicable one.

HARRIER *n.* A small hound used in Britain for hunting hares. In similar fashion, the good people of the old country use foxhounds to hunt foxes, ferrets to hunt rabbits, German shepherds to hunt criminals, buckhounds to hunt stags, dukes to hunt pheasants, and basset hounds to hunt badgers. A moment's reflection will reveal that, seen from the point of view of the systems analyst, all this is extremely wasteful of resources. What we have here, in essence, is a series of one-to-one relationships. Now imagine the individual components set out vertically in a single chain. We would have a self-contained and fully integrated system in which German shepherds hunted criminals, criminals hunted dukes, dukes hunted buckhounds, buckhounds hunted foxhounds, foxhounds hunted basset hounds, basset hounds hunted stags, stags hunted foxes, foxes hunted badgers, badgers hunted ferrets, ferrets hunted rabbits, and rabbits hunted pheasants. No duplication of effort, no wasted resources; another triumph for the systems approach!

HEBETATE *v.* To grow dull or stupid. 'Remember,' you say sententiously to the Seventh Grade as they struggle with their arithmetic test, 'he who hebetates is last.' The verb can also be transitive, meaning to make someone else grow dull or stupid – a sense of which it is hard to conceive an example, except perhaps for the action upon the mind of prolonged exposure to radio talk shows. The noun is *hebetude*.

HENCHPERSON *n.* Close and trusty follower. This new word has been created by the author to replace its *sexist* (q.v.) and thus outdated equivalent, *henchman*, which had gradually acquired, over the years, a *pejorative* (q.v.) flavor. Villains have henchmen; heroes have right-hand men – or, more properly, right-hand people.

HENOTHEISM *n.* (i) Belief that God is a hen; (ii) belief that Henny Youngman is God; (iii) belief in one God without necessarily accepting that he or she is the only God. Of these three meanings, the author much prefers the first; the last is, however, the only one accepted by other lexicographers, despite the fact that it seems intrinsically the least convincing of the three.

HETEROSEXUAL *a.* A word that has, paradoxically, come into its own along with increasing acceptance by society of the behavior described by its antonym. Its modern usage is thus essentially defensive. When in receipt of homosexual advances, the correct response is, 'Sir [or madam], I am strictly heterosexual.' n.b. Not to be confused, especially in the context just mentioned, with *bisexual*.

HEURISTIC *a.* Serving to promote discovery. Sometimes used as *highfalutin* (q.v.) jargon to describe the so-called 'discovery method' in education, through which children supposedly find things out for themselves instead of being taught. Teacher trainees – or teacher education students, as they are now called – never find out about the heuristic method by themselves; they are taught about it by their lecturers.

HIGHFALUTIN *a.* High-flown, pretentious (of language). As, for instance, the words in this book. Other lexicographers give the ending *-ing* for this word as an alternative, but the properly highfalutin usage is the ending *-in* – without, be it noted, any following apostrophe. The etymology is obscure, but the author likes to think that the original derivation may lie in the verb 'to faloot,' from the vigorous patois spoken by the early settlers of the Mississippi region – even though the meaning is too indelicate, and its application to the present case too preposterous, for this possibility to be explored in depth in the present work.

HINNY *n.* The offspring of a female donkey and a male horse. Less common than *mule* (the offspring of a male donkey and a female horse). The words *tigon* and *liger* have been coined to describe the outcome of an unlikely liaison between a lion and a tiger. *Catalo* means the offspring of a cow and a buffalo; *jumart* that of a cow and a donkey; *yakalo* that of yak and a catalo; and *zebrula* that of a zebra and a horse.

HIRCINE *a.* Goatish, lewd. (See *abecedarian insult, an.*)

HOMEOPATH, NATURAPATH, OSTEOPATH, ETC. *n.* So called because of the pathologically gullible, and pathologically talkative, nature of their patients. *Path-* from the Greek *pathos*: suffering, affliction. If you suffer from the affliction of a close friend or colleague who devotes a considerable part of his conversation to lengthy accounts of mysterious ailments cured miraculously by a rather wonderful little *-path* of some kind whom he has discovered in a nearby suburb, the correct approach is to say: 'I'm interested to hear you say that, because only the other day I discovered a rather wonderful little psychopath who I think could do wonders for you.'

HOMUNCULUS *n.* Manikin. A wonderfully offensive word for the modern miss to use in addressing any male of less than average height, especially in the process of deterring unwelcome advances on his part. Happily, there appears to be no feminine counterpart.

HYPERTOKENISM *n.* Appointment of a female member of a minority group to a government committee. (See *tokenism.*)

I

IDIOTROPIC *a*. Turned in upon oneself, introspective. The same sense is apparent in *idioticon* (the private possession of someone, something peculiarly the property of its owner) and *idiotropian* (a characteristic peculiar to the individual). In all these cases the presence of the letter *t* is misleading; the meaning is not as in *idiot* but as in *idiosyncrasy*. Nonetheless, it is possible to derive a certain amount of quiet pleasure from the suggestion of ambiguity inherent in these terms.

IGNOTUM PER IGNOTIUS *n*. An explanation which is even more obscure than the thing it purports to explain. Literally, 'the unknown by the more unknown.' There are two forms – the unintended and the intended. For an example of the former, see the printed instructions for setting up and operating your wife's sewing machine. The art of the latter should be materially advanced by the lore contained in this book, and could well be cultivated by the Superior Person along with the arts of *charientism* (q.v.) and *parisology* (q.v.).

ILK *n.* The final and perfect pejorative-in-a-nutshell.

IMAGO *n.* The final and perfect stage of an insect after it has gone through all its metamorphoses. For example, a butterfly. 'Ah,' you exclaim, as your sister at last emerges from the bathroom, fully decorated and ready to receive her latest *fungible* (q.v.), 'the ultimate imago!'

IMPALEMENT *n.* Transfixion. Commonly applied now to the transfixion of drunken drivers by steering wheels, but originally the only sedentary form of capital punishment until the electric chair, involving a pointed stake, or *pale* (the latter being the predecessor of our innocent paling fence). 'Beyond the pale' meant 'on the wrong side of the fence' in Ireland, i.e., in the part not under English rule. For an account of a particularly nasty nonsedentary impalement, read Hume's sympathetic and enlightened account of the reign of Edward II.

IMPECCABLE *a.* Flawless; not able to be faulted. Curiously, although the original sense was 'not susceptible to sin,' the term has come to be used less in relation to human character and morals than in relation to human aesthetics. Thus, 'her appearance was impeccable'; or 'a person of impeccable taste.' (As, for instance, the person who gave you this book for your birthday.)

INDEFECTIBLE *a.* Not capable of being faulted; not liable to defect, flaw, or failure.

INDIFFERENTISM *n.* Indifference as a basic principle or guiding spirit in religious matters. The only religious persuasion (if that is not too inappropriate a word) in whose name no one has ever been imprisoned, tortured, or killed; hence widely condemned by earnest believers. The most disarming and charming of prejudices. 'I regret to announce that the meetings of the Indifferentism Society for the remainder of the year have had to be canceled because of lack of interest among members.'

INEFFABLE *a.* Unutterable. Only two things are ineffable – a bore, and bliss. 'Sir, you are an ineffable bore.' Indeed, bores are seldom anything other than ineffable. Bliss, however, can alternatively be *unalloyed*.

INELUCTABLE *a.* Inescapable. Note that this is not a synonym for *unavoidable, inexorable,* or *inevitable*. The sense of the Latin root is 'that cannot be struggled out of.' Thus the conversation of an *ineffable* (q.v.) bore may be avoidable but, if not in fact avoided, may prove ineluctable; whereas the day-long television coverage of a golf tournament may be unavoidable, without being ineluctable.

INEXPLICABLE *a.* Unexplainable. To be preferred because of the effect that can be achieved by pronouncing it, as did Olivier in *Hamlet* ('inexplicable dumb shows and noise'), with the accent not on the third syllable but on the *second*. Note, however, that this requires intensive practice.

INFRASTRUCTURE *n.* A modern piece of cant, of no discernibly useful meaning, much employed by jargonizing social scientists. Respond to its use with the same technique recommended for *structure* (q.v.).

INGRAVESCENT *a.* Growing worse or more severe. A medical term used of illnesses, a patient's morbid condition or disease, etc. Suggested for use instead as a faintly *pejorative* (q.v.) descriptive for your less savory acquaintances. 'How's Isidore these days?' 'Oh, ingravescent, I'm afraid – distinctly ingravescent.'

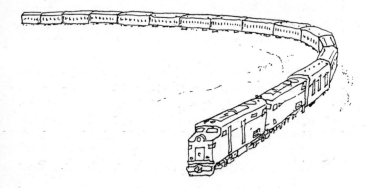

interminable

INSOLATION *n.* Exposure to the rays of the sun. A useful substitute for *sunbathing*. 'I'll be taking a long lunch-hour today, Mr. Fernberd, if that's all right with you – I'm overdue for my insolation treatment.'

INSPISSATE *v.* To thicken, especially a liquid, by evaporation. 'Excuse me for a moment while I inspissate the soup.'

INTERMINABLE *a.* Apparently incapable of being brought to an end. As, for example, a long-playing record of Scottish country dance music, or of the piano rags of Scott Joplin.

INTUMESCENCE *n.* Swelling. Why refer to the high tide, or to the rising tide, when you can use a phrase as glorious as 'the intumescence of the tide'?

IRREDENTIST *n.* One whose faction advocates the annexation of foreign territory because of its historic links with one's own country. When your beloved's mother icily eyes your faded jeans upon your being introduced to her for the first time, and asks you what you do for a living, you could say that you are an irredentist, and that you don't actually work anymore. She will assume you to be a wealthy orthodontist, and your romance will prosper.

ISOMORPHIC *a.* Being of the same shape and general appearance, but not of the same ancestry, as something else. As, for example, any pet dog and its owner – more especially any show-dog and its owner.

ITAIITAI *n.* A bone disease caused by cadmium. Said to be derived from the Japanese equivalent for 'Ouch, ouch!' The interest of this to the lexicographer lies in the possibility of forming similar neologisms in English to provide more directly meaningful names for other diseases and conditions. Thus, 'Eek, eek!' for arachniphobia; 'Er, er' for aphasia; 'Unh, unh!' for constipation; 'Ha, ha!' for alopecia; 'Oh, no!' for impotence; and so on.

ITHYPHALLIC *a.* Obscure, impure, indecent. From the phallus carried in Bacchic festivals. The slight similarity of the prefix to *ichthyo* (to do with fish) may enable you to venture upon some little *jeu d'esprit* of your own devising with your Aunt Ethel who keeps tropical fish. In fact, some of the doings of her Egyptian Mouthbreeders, her Kissing Gouramis, or her Slippery Dicks may well deserve the above epithet.

J

JACKANAPES *n.* A silly, impertinent monkey of a fellow. Authorities differ on the derivation. The Concise Oxford Dictionary links the names of Jack Napes and William de la Pole, Duke of Suffolk in the fifteenth century, whose badge was a clog and chain of the kind used for a tame ape. Brewer offers two possibilities – Jack of Apes and Jack-apes (the latter on the analogy of jackass). Webster suggests Jack of Naples, the word *jack* in this case meaning monkey. Goes nicely with *popinjay* and *coxcomb*. When you finally get through to the general manager of the department store with your complaint, you begin by explaining that you have already spoken to a jackanapes, a popinjay, and a coxcomb. You may use the same remark even if you have spoken only to one person.

JACTATION *n.* Boasting, bragging. A specialized – indeed highly specialized – variant is *jactitation*, as in 'jactitation of marriage': falsely putting it about that you are married to a particular person. Both words may be of use in wedding-reception speech-making, but the author leaves the specifics of this to the reader.

JAPE *n.* A prank or joke. The word has overtones of English public (i.e., private) school humor and the writings of Frank Richards. Should be used in relation to the more tiresome antics of your office comedian. 'This is hardly the time for one of your junior-high japes, Plunkett.'

JAWBONING *n.* Making use of the government's authority and prestige to persuade business and labor to moderate their demands in the national interest. Comparable with an antelope's using its authority and prestige to persuade a lion and a tiger to moderate their demands in the interests of environmentalism. Hence, no doubt, the reference to the jawbone, which is all that remains of the antelope.

JEJUNE *a.* Short on worthwhile content. A perfect example of the Superior Word, were it not for the inhibitions aroused even in Superior People by the prospect of having to pronounce it not only correctly but casually.

JOBATION *n.* A long, tedious scolding; a lengthy reprimand; a tirade. When you find yourself on the receiving end of yet another insultingly patronizing suggestion from Colonel Carstairs about how you could improve the appearance of your yard, you say: 'By gosh, old boy, that's awfully nice of you! Look – next time you come around I really *must* remember to get my wife to give you one of her jobations.'

jugulation

JUGULATION *n.* (i) Interruption of the progress of a disease by dire measures; (ii) throat-cutting. The second use makes this a rather nice companion piece for *defenestration* (q.v.).

K

KAKISTOCRACY *n.* Government by the worst citizens. For reasons which can only be speculated upon, there is no word for government by the best citizens. *Aristarchy* means government by the best-qualified persons, but the latter are not necessarily the best – indeed, an aristarchy could quite conceivably be a kakistocracy.

KEDOGENOUS *a.* Brought about by worry, or anxiety. Useful for excuses. 'I'm awfully sorry, darling, but I'm afraid I seem to have another of my kedogenous headaches.'

KERATIN *n.* A substance found in hair, or fingernails. The author would like to be more explicit, but none of his references identify the actual substance. He can only assume it to be sump oil, sandwich spread, or garden compost.

KICKSHAW *n.* A gimcrack gewgaw. Three weird and wonderful words that merit a wider currency in the

75

spoken language. *Kickshaw* derives from the French *quelque chose*; *gimcrack* possibly from *gim* (pert) and *crack* (boaster); and *gewgaw* possibly from *give-gove* (present). All mean trinket.

KINDERGRAPH *n.* Photograph of a child. A word which, unlike *kindergarten*, has passed into obsolescence, but which undoubtedly merits revivification in view of the widespread occurrence of the phenomenon in question.

KINETOSIS *n.* A fancy name for travel sickness.

KINKAJOU *n.* A furry, domesticatable mammal with a prehensile tail. Rather sweet as an outré term of endearment for your beloved. 'Come, my little kinkajou.'

KNICKERBOCKERS *n.* Loose-fitting pants gathered in at the knee. For some reason as yet unfathomed by the author, the enunciation aloud of the abbreviated form of the word, *knickers*, will make any Englishman laugh uncontrollably. The reaction is invariable, and indeed can be made use of by medical men as an alternative to the patellar reflex in testing the neurological system of an Englishman whose legs have been amputated above the knee. The reflex does not occur in Americans or Australians, and appears to have deep-laid ethnic origins.

KOPOPHOBIA *n.* Fear of exhaustion. Otherwise known as Lexicographer's Curse.

L

LABILE *a.* Unstable, liable to change. Essentially this is a technical term from the realms of chemistry, but it has been appropriated by social scientists who operate on the principle that the use of the esoteric term instead of the familiar will lend their writings an aura of scientific prestige (see *paradigm*). The term is thus used to refer to personality or emotion. It is, as it happens, rather nicely suggestive of a combination of *labial* (of the lips; involving compression of the lips) and *nubile* (marriageable – generally referring to the physical condition of young women). Rather a pity, then, that the real meaning is temperamental, moody.

LABROSE *a.* Thick-lipped. (See *abecedarian insult, an.*)

LAPIDATE *v.* Stone to death. When your mother's well-meaning but interventionist crony Mrs. Planterbox remarks, for the fourteenth time, what a pity it is that your children spend all their time reading instead of having a *proper* hobby, you explain that they used to take an interest in lapidation but have had difficulty in finding a suitable subject – perhaps she might find the time to oblige?

LEMAN *n. Paramour* (q.v.); lover; inamorata (or, for that matter, inamorato – but the female sense, of mistress, has for some reason become the more common in recent times). May be pronounced lemon, leeman, or even, according to one of the author's sources, layman. The first and third of these pronunciations offer obvious opportunities.

LESION *n.* The Superior Person's word for a scratch, cut, bruise, abrasion, sore, or pimple.

LETHOLOGICA and **LETHONOMIA** *n.* The former is the inability to recall the right word, the latter the inability to recall the right name. The reader who suffers from either (or, like the author, both) of these conditions should practice saying, 'Excuse my lethologica/lethonomia'; this is distinctly preferable to saying, 'It's on the tip of my tongue ...,' but, unfortunately, also distinctly harder – in fact, almost impossible for one who suffers from the condition(s) in question.

LEXIPHANIC *a.* Given to the use of pretentious terminology, such as the word *lexiphanic*.

LIMACEOUS *a.* Sluglike, having to do with slugs. 'Keep your hands to yourself, you limaceous endomorph!'

LIMPOPO *n.* A river, otherwise known (for obvious reasons) as the Crocodile River, in southern Africa.

Alternatively (without the initial capital), the avocado, a pear-shaped tropical fruit, otherwise known as the alligator pear. This usage derives not from the connection between Crocodile River and alligator pear but from the writings of Kipling, whose phrase 'the great, grey, green, greasy Limpopo' is so exactly indicative of the nature of the fruit. The avocado had just been introduced into London at the time Kipling was writing his *Jungle Book*, and his description of the Limpopo is said to have been devised as a private joke for the amusement of two friends in whose presence he had first sampled the fruit in question and found it quite disgusting.

LIPPITUDE *n.* A bleary-eyed condition. Goes well with *lucifugous* (q.v.) in descriptions of morning-after symptoms.

LUBRICITY *n.* Lasciviousness, lewdness, oiliness. A marvelously nasty word. Can be used nonpejoratively to mean smoothness, or slipperiness, e.g., of fate – but why waste such an insinuative word on such mundane uses?

LUCIFUGOUS *a.* Avoiding daylight. A botanical term. 'I'm afraid John's not up yet, Mrs. Applecore; he overindulged somewhat last night, and the poor dear is distinctly lucifugous this morning.'

LUCRIPETOUS *a.* Money-hungry. Goes rather nicely with *nummamorous* (q.v.). Both words are suitable for muttered aspersions upon the motives of used-car salesmen, estate agents, funeral directors, and their ilk, when in their presence.

LUCUBRATION *n.* Laborious intellectual effort; alternatively, a literary composition of a heavy-handed, overly elaborate nature, produced by dint of much burning of the midnight oil. Definitely pejorative in impact, even without allowing for its faint overtones of certain intrinsically unpleasant words such as *lugubrious* and *lubricious*.

lustration

LUMINARY *n.* A person of great intellectual or spiritual stature; one who spreads the light of truth and beauty around him. As, for instance, the late Albert Schweitzer. Note that not all dignitaries are luminaries, and not all luminaries are dignitaries.

LUPINE *a.* Having the characteristics of a wolf. Everyone is familiar with the use of *feline, canine,* or *leonine* to describe human traits; in practice, *lupine* may well be more useful, as may *vulpine* (foxlike) and *hircine* (goatish).

LUSTRATION *n.* Ritual purification by ceremonial washing or sacrifice. Literally, illumination or making shiny. A nice grandiloquism for spring-cleaning.

LUSUS NATURAE *n.* A freak of nature; an abnormality. Literally, a sport of Nature. 'And now, fellow pupils, it is my privilege to welcome, on behalf of the student body, our most distinguished alumnus – a *lusus naturae* if ever there was one – Colonel ...'

M

MACARONIC *n.* Every British schoolboy knows A.D. Godley's little poem which begins: 'What is this that roareth thus? / Can it be a motor bus? / Yes, the smell and hideous hum / *Indicat motorem bum! ...*' The Superior Person also knows that the proper name for this kind of poem is *macaronic*; that is, a poem of a burlesque nature in which a modern vernacular language is intermixed with Latin words or inflections. The derivation appears to be from *macaroon*, which formerly meant not only the sweet biscuit of that name but also (and indeed more so) a coarse, doltish buffoon – or, as we would say today, a crazy mixed-up kid. If you are lucky enough to come across your *galootish* (q.v.) nephew Clint engaged in the consumption of a macaroon, you could quietly make a cryptic observation about the persistence of cannibalism in modern society.

MACERATE *v.* Soften by soaking. 'Oh, Mother, it really is *too* much; Richard's at it again – I wish you could stop him. I can't get into the bathroom. The door's locked, and he's been in there for half an hour now; I'm sure he must be macerating.'

MACROLOGY *n.* Long and tiresome talk; a *nimiety* (q.v.) of words. A macrologist is thus a bore. When cornered by such a one at a party, you firmly steer him, still talking, to the nearest professor of organic chemistry. 'I'd like you to meet one of our leading macrologists,' you say, and leave the two together, having just given the good professor the impression that he has just been introduced to a specialist in a new field of microbiology.

MADEFY *v.* To dampen, wet, or moisten. You arrive, somewhat bedraggled, at the dinner party being given in your honor by your fiancée's mother, having been caught in the rain en route. She commiserates with you, but you brightly respond before the assembled group: 'Well, it could have been worse; I'm madefied, but at least I'm not *macerating* [q.v.].'

MAMMIFEROUS *a.* Having breasts. Strictly speaking, all mammals, whether male or female, but, needless to say, more commonly applied in relation to the latter. Like *steatopygous* (q.v.), a word that is not likely to be readily grasped by the unprepared listener. You have arrived at a seaside resort for a bachelor's holiday with your mother; en route to the hotel your taxi passes the local headquarters of the Young Women's Christian Association. 'Excuse me, Mama,' you say excitedly, 'but I think I have spotted some specimens of the mammifera' – and, seizing your butterfly net, you leap out of the cab and send it, complete with mother, on ahead of you.

MANQUÉ *a.* Having not achieved a condition pretended to, desired, or deemed suited for. Said of an individual who has failed (for want of opportunity, capacity, volition, or endeavor) to attain a position or role for which his affinity is now apparent from his ersatz performance or from his obsessive speech or behavior. Note that the term does not mean (as might have been supposed from its French derivation) simply the absence or lack of the quality in question. It implies a desire for it, and a longing or regret for what might have been. Thus every forty-year-old layman, but no forty-year-old priest, might be described as a voluptuary manqué.

MARCHPANE *n.* Never say *marzipan*; always say *marchpane*. The two words are identical in meaning. *Marchpane*, the less common and therefore the preferable one, is derived from the French; *marzipan*, from the German.

MATRIX *n.* Like *structure* (q.v.) and *parameter*, a term whose constant transmigration between the physical and the social sciences has led to all kinds of misuse and confusion. The primary meaning of *matrix* is a womb, or mold, in which something is engendered – the derivation is from the Latin word for mother. A secondary meaning, in mathematics, is a square or rectangular array of symbols. When a social scientist uses the term in any other sense, always ask immediately: 'Pardon me, but when you say "matrix," do you really mean, in this context, "parameter"?' When he uses the word *parameter* in any sense other than one of its technical mathematical senses, immediately ask: 'Pardon me, but when you say "parameter," do you really mean, in this context, "matrix"?'

MEDULLA OBLONGATA *n.* The backside of the brain, where it tapers off into the spinal cord. Claimed by plausible neurologists to be a kind of main junction where nerve pathways cross and change direction. Claimed also to be the seat of control for breathing, circulation, and swallowing. Certainly the seat of a distinctive form of pounding agony induced by the consumption of large quantities of tequila the night before. Alternatively (but now obsolescent), a musical term meaning 'with accompaniment played on the medulla.' The medulla was a specially muted lute, developed in the sixteenth century by the notoriously underhanded troubadour Felix von Furchteviel, from whose name comes our word *furtive*.

MEGAPOD *a.* Having large feet. Useful if you wish to show consideration for the feelings of a police officer, while keeping the conversation on a factual level.

MEPHITIC or **MEPHITICAL** *a.* Stinking, noxious, *noisome* (q.v.). Strictly speaking, foul or poisonous exhalations from the earth or other low-level source. See Frazer's account of the worship of mephitic vapors in *The Golden Bough*, from which the following: 'The ancients regarded the vents from which they [i.e., noxious vapors] were discharged as entrances to the infernal regions. In Italy the vapors were personified as a goddess, who bore the name of Mefitis. She had a temple in the famous valley of Amsanctus in the land of the Hirpini, where the exhalations, supposed to be the breath of Pluto himself, were of so deadly a character that all who set foot on the spot died. The pool is now called Mefite and the holes Mefitinelle. On the other side of the pool is a smaller pond called the Coccaio, or cauldron, because it appears to be perpetually boiling. Thick masses of mephitic vapor, visible a hundred yards off, float in rapid undulations on its surface. The exhalations given off by these waters are sometimes fatal, especially when they are borne on a high wind. But as the carbonic acid gas does not naturally rise more than two or three feet from the ground, it is possible in calm weather to walk around the pools, though to stoop is difficult and to fall would be dangerous.' *Mephitic* is thus a term that should not be applied to an aroma that is met with well above ground level, such as your lanky cousin Gilbert's aftershave lotion, but rather to the effluvia encountered during your annual clean-out of the grease trap behind the garage, a chance encounter with a dachshund, or a trip in an elevator with a short person who is smoking a pipe (see *suffumigate*).

MERKIN *n.* A pubic wig for women, or, to quote Grose's *Dictionary of the Vulgar Tongue,* 'counterfeit hair for women's privy parts.' Do not ask the author to explain this. The lexicographer's duty is merely to record. To others remains it to remark, with Ambrose Bierce, 'Can such things be?'

MERRYTHOUGHT *n.* Wishbone. A delightful archaism.

MEZZOTINT *n.* A kind of engraving made by first roughening the plate and then either scraping away or leaving the rough surface, thus producing various shading effects in the final print. Knowledge of the word is necessary for an understanding of the ghost stories of M. R. James; but don't bother going into the Happie Valley Arte and Crafte Gallerie and asking to see their mezzotints, as this could lead only to confusion.

MIASMA *n.* Noxious atmosphere or emanations. The proper appellation for the air inside a pseudo-French restaurant; in genuine French restaurants garlic is used in only *some* of the dishes. A word wonderfully evocative of stupefying mists, curling heavily and dankly around. Useful not only on entering restaurants but also on looking into younger brothers' bedrooms.

MICROHENRY *n.* Unit of measurement of electrical inductance equal to one millionth of a henry. The author's sources do not make it clear whether the definition is applicable to any henry; presumably it is, but in the absence of a clear reference on the matter, he suggests to readers that they interpret the relationship as applying to an average henry. A microlambert, incidentally, is a unit of brightness, equal to one millionth of a lambert.

MOLIMINOUS *a.* Momentous; of great bulk or importance; laborious in the execution and of great consequence in the finished form. As, for example, the present book. Generally applied to objects or enterprises, but could be jocularly applied to your employer, your mother-in-law, your bank manager, etc., as appropriate.

MOUNTEBANK *n.* Spectacular charlatan. One who, in olden times, mounted a banco, or bench, to attract the attention of his audience. A little-known synonym is *saltimbanco* – the derivation being based on the same principle, *saltatio* being the Latin for a jump or leap. The difficulty of forming new words as easily as this today can be gauged from the fact that the charlatan who wishes to display his wares now does not mount a bench, but solicits a guest appearance on a daytime television talk show.

MUCILAGE *n.* The Superior Person does not use gum, glue, or paste. He or she uses mucilage.

MULIEBRITY *n.* The quality of being womanly; softness, femininity. The female equivalent of virility. Not to be confused with *mulishness*.

MULTILOQUOUS *a.* Very talkative. Goes well with *macrologist* (q.v.). *Pauciloquous* is the antonym.

MUNDUNGUS *n.* Bad-smelling tobacco. Not, as one might expect, from *dung*, but from *mondongo* (Spanish for tripe). An archaism largely unknown today, but worth reviving as a synonym for pipe tobacco. When your pipe-smoking colleague enters your room, you say: 'Ah, still using the old mundungus, eh?' He cuts his visit short in order to go and look up the word while he can still remember it. Meanwhile you turn to your office copy of this book, to find a suitable word for his next visit.

MUSSITATION *n.* Murmuring, grumbling. The sounds of a sulking teenager.

MYSTAGOGUE *n.* One who instructs in mystical or arcane lore and doctrines. Originally one who prepared candidates for initiation into the Eleusinian mysteries or other secret religious rites of the ancients. Nowadays, perhaps, one who demonstrates electronic organs in music shops.

N

NAPIFORM *a.* Shaped like a turnip. (See *abecedarian insult, an.*)

NATTERJACK *n.* A curiously warty, pop-eyed toad, with a bright yellow line down its back. The word is useful for the simple Insult Concealed.

NAUMACHIA *n.* A mock naval battle presented as a spectacle in ancient Rome. In modern times, a nice grandiloquism for water polo.

NAUPATHIA *n.* The recommended grandiloquism for seasickness. (See also *kinetosis.*)

NEFANDOUS *a.* Unspeakable, unutterable. Usually associated with a noun indicative of wickedness: nefandous villainy, nefandous lechery, nefandous pipe -smoking, etc. The author prefers to associate it with *nefarious*, and speak of nefandous nefariousness. This is even more confusing than it sounds, because the etymology of the two words overlaps. The former comes from the Latin *ne* (not) and *fari* (to speak), and the latter from the Latin *ne* (not) and *fas* (divine law) – but *fas* itself is in turn related to *fari*. You might like to take time out to explain this to the listener when you use either word – especially if he is a pipe-smoker, since the chances are that before you have finished he will simply go away.

NEPENTHE *n.* Something that brings forgetfulness of sorrow and suffering. The perfect brand name for a new liqueur.

NEPHELIGENOUS *a.* Producing clouds of smoke. From the Greek word for cloud. A suitably stern epithet for a pipe-smoker. Nephelology is the study of clouds. A nephelolater is an admirer of clouds. A nephelosphere is a vaporous, cloudy envelope surrounding a heavenly body. 'Ah, I thought I recognized your nephelosphere,' you say to Gloria as she enters the room, fresh from a session with her hairspray.

NEPOTATION *n.* Prodigality; extravagance, squandering one's money on riotous living. 'Well, Headmaster, since you ask, it had always been my ambition to go in for nepotation when I leave school; but in the light of my examination results I suppose Quantity Surveying *would* be more appropriate.' Not to be confused with nepotism, which is favoritism to relatives – originally fondness for nephews, specifically papal fondness for illegitimate sons euphemistically referred to as nephews and advantaged by the bestowal of papal patronage in various ways.

NESCIENCE *n.* Lack of knowledge, ignorance. A word of which – unlike *prescience* (foreknowledge) – most people are nescient. Hence useful for the Insult Concealed. 'My dear, I can only marvel at the extent of your nescience.'

NIDIFICATE *v.* To build a nest. You settle down in the quietness of the theater to enjoy the opening dream sequence of *Wild Strawberries*. From the seat in front of you comes an insistent crackling and rustling of candy wrappings. 'Usher!' you call out in a loud voice, 'I think the woman in front of me is nidificating in her seat!'

NIKHEDONIA *n.* The pleasure and satisfaction derived from the anticipation of success. A harmless indulgence, and a prudent one too, since success comes only to some but nikhedonia is freely available to all. 'Off to golf so early, darling? Hadn't you better have your little nikhedonia session first? You know how badly you play when your gummata are troubling you.'

NIMIETY *n.* Excess, extravagance, surfeit. The adjective is *nimious*. According to Webster, Coleridge said: 'There is a nimiety, a too-muchness, in all Germans.' In modern times, perhaps American tourists might be substituted for Germans; but, be that as it may, Coleridge's *mot* does lead us to the possibility of using *nimious* in the sense of 'too much.' 'Really, Roger, you simply are nimious.'

NOCENT and **NOCUOUS** *a.* Two never-used words with the same meaning – harmful. A moment's reflection will reveal that they provide the basis for those much more common words *innocent* and *innocuous*. It is comforting to discover that our civilization has found more use for the latter two terms than for the former two. On the other hand, it has found more use for *uncouth* than for *couth*. Perhaps this simply means that, for deep-laid psychological or linguistic reasons, we have a natural preference for the use of words which have been negatived by prefix. If so, the author may have high hopes for the success of his own neologism, *unundulating* (q.v.).

NODOSE *a.* Knobbly, knotty. The noun is *nodosity*. When you express concern over Uncle Henry's *genual* (q.v.) nodosity, you are in fact merely commenting upon his knobby knees.

NOISOME *a.* Noxious, smelly, nasty. Note that this is definitely *not* a synonym for *noisy*. Much quiet satisfaction can be derived from putting your head around the door of your younger brother's room, saying, 'It's rather noisome in here, isn't it?' and hearing him turn down his stereo as you go on your way.

NONE *pron.* Not any. The interest here lies in the question, much debated in the past, of whether the word is singular or plural. The argument used to be that since *one* was singular, and since *none* was derived from *no one*, then *none* should have a singular verb. In practice, of course, it is used equally if not more freely with a plural verb. In any event, the argument is absurd, since the word refers neither to a single entity nor to multiple entities; it refers to a nullity, and hence calls for the development by a creative linguist of an entirely new conjugative inflection. Unfortunately, 'creative linguist' is an *oxymoron* (q.v.).

NOSOPOETIC *a.* Producing disease, unhygienic; infected. 'Ah, how perfectly nosopoetic!' is the proper exclamation for you to employ when the wealthy Pimplewickers, of whose possessions you are already insanely jealous, proudly show off to you their new fishpond/seaside cottage/sunken garden/bathroom tiles/Samoyed dog/Abyssinian cat/antique Persian rug, etc., etc.

NOYADE *n.* Mass execution by drowning, as in revolutionary France. The technique was invented by a 'monster of ferocity' (to quote Maunder) named Carrier, and involved some one hundred and fifty people being shut up in the hold of a ship, which was then scuttled in the Loire. This was called, rather delightfully, 'Carrier's Vertical Deportation.' 'Have a good old noyade, now,' you cry out to the Seventh Grade as they depart in the school bus for their swimming lesson. Knowing your penchant for esoteric vocabulary, they smile tolerantly and turn their full attention to the task of *defenestrating* (q.v.) the phys. ed. teacher.

NUGATORY *a.* Of no value, trifling, insubstantial, pointless. Unfavorable criticism of the present book could properly be so characterized.

NULLIBIETY *n.* State of being nowhere. A word for which it would at first appear difficult to conceive any practical use; but no incomprehensible word can be completely useless. 'And in conclusion, Stafford, on behalf of everyone here, may I heartily wish you an unimpaired nullibiety.' Or: 'Yes, when there's a job to be done around the house, I know I can rely absolutely on Stafford's nullibiety.'

NUMMAMOROUS *a.* Money-loving. From the Latin *nummus*, a coin. (See also *lucripetous*.)

NYMPHOLEPSY *n.* *Not* a convulsive condition of nubiles, but a passionate longing for something unattainable. A sufferer is a *nympholept*. The condition is named after the supposed result of looking upon a nymph, an act which, according to legend, produced a frenzy of enthusiastic emotion in the looker-upon. In modern parlance, you could use the term to refer to the passion of a vintage-car enthusiast for an impossibly expensive Bugatti; or of a bibliophile for a Shakespeare First Folio; or, let's face it, of a voluptuary *manqué* (q.v.) for a nymphomaniac.

O

OBJURGATE *v.* Chide, scold, upbraid vehemently. The third of the three great principles inculcated in young ladies by finishing schools: Conjugate, Subjugate, Objurgate.

OBLOQUY *n.* (i) Public condemnation, and/or the ensuing disgrace; (ii) opprobrious language. A word that hangs uncertainly between *odium* and *opprobrium*, leaning more toward the latter but sometimes simply meaning scornful and accusing language. The author would try to set forth a sentence using all three, for illustrative purposes, were it not for the odium, the obloquy, the opprobrium, and indeed the objurgation that would be his lot if he succeeded only in effecting an obfuscation.

ochlophobia

OCHLOPHOBIA *n.* The obsessive fear of crowds. The most understandable of phobias.

ODIUM *n.* The burden of the distastefulness of a particular act. Generally borne or incurred by a person associated with the act in question. Not to be confused with *opprobrium*, the disgrace incurred as a consequence of the act. The difficulty of dissociating the two meanings lies in the fact that the two penalties they represent are generally incurred at the same time, through the same act, and both involve the disapproval of others. The emphasis in the case of *odium*, however, is upon the intrinsic hatefulness of the act itself; in the case of *opprobrium*, upon the actual reproaches incurred. There is generally a time-sequence element involved also. As you prepare to fling the tomato at the old lady in the wheelchair, you are already steeling yourself to bear the odium of the act; as you fling it, you incur the odium; the opprobrium of the bystanders follows a split second later.

ODONTALGIA and **ODONTIASIS** *n.* Toothache and teething, respectively. Your own odontalgia, or your child's odontiasis, might usefully be mentioned when excusing yourself from coming into the office until later on in the morning. But not too bluntly. Say, in a diffident and strained tone of voice: 'I'm having a spot of my old trouble again, I'm afraid – you know, the, er ...' (here lower your voice to a confidential whisper) '... odontalgia. I'd sooner the others didn't know, incidentally.'

OENOMEL *n.* (i) A beverage made of wine and honey; thence, (ii) something that blends strength with sweetness. A female wrestler, perhaps?

OLEAGINOUS *a.* Oily. The personal manner of actors appearing in television commercials for banks and finance companies.

OLIGOPHAGOUS *a.* Eating only a few particular kinds of food. This is the recommended word for use in those embarrassing situations when your hostess serves up for your four-year-old son a main course consisting largely of something which is *anathema* (q.v.) to him. As soon as you sense the *alliaceous miasma* (q.v.), you say, apologetically: 'I'm a little embarrassed to have to confess this, but I'm afraid he has an oligophagous condition; I wonder if you have any dry biscuits – or perhaps something else a little, er, plainer?' Used with sufficient finesse, this technique can lead to his being presented with a plateful of sausage rolls.

OLIGOPHRENIA *n.* Feeblemindedness; extreme mental retardation. (See *abecedarian insult, an.*)

ONIOMANIA *n.* An irresistible urge to buy things. The condition is generally found in association with penury; where it is not, it soon will be, especially as oniomaniacs, like *thermanasthesiacs* (q.v.), often marry each other.

ONTOLOGICAL *a.* Having to do with the science or study of essence or being. The ontological argument for the existence of God, as developed by Anselm, is that the very concept of a perfect being leads inevitably to the existence of that being, since a nonexistent perfect being's perfection would be made imperfect by its nonexistence. The same argument may, of course, be used to prove the existence of the perfect hamburger, though it was not so used by Anselm. There are two reasons for equipping yourself with this word. First, to armor yourself psychologically against the pretensions of existentialists – progressive theologians, educationists, and their ilk – who use the term indiscriminately, waving it over their monologues like a magic wand that is supposed to turn words into arguments. Secondly, to pepper your own conversation with it, for the purpose of obscuring issues, impressing undergraduates of the opposite sex, and confusing social scientists. Thus: 'Ontologically speaking, ...' (this can lead into virtually *any* remark); 'there's a certain ontological force about what you say, I admit, but …'; etc., etc.

ONYMOUS *a.* Not anonymous. A rather sweet little word: 'And I'd appreciate it if you'd stop sending me onymous letters!' you call out after your unwanted suitor as he walks away down the crowded main street, crestfallen from your latest rebuff.

OPERCULUM *n.* Organ of a plant or animal that acts as a covering or lid. Could be used to describe the hat worn by one of those men who *never* go anywhere, or do anything, hatless. Plainclothes policemen are traditionally operculiferous. An even more extreme case is that of the man who wears his hat while actually driving his car. Be warned: it is an observed fact that operculiferous drivers are dangerous. More so even than pipe-smoking drivers. If you notice that the driver of the car in front of yours, or behind it, is *both* operculiferous and pipe-smoking, then pull to the side of the road immediately, and wait until it is safe to proceed.

OPISTHENAR *n.* Back of the hand. In pronouncing, the stress is on the *pis*. 'Mom,' you cry out from the bathroom at a quarter to seven in the morning, when she is only just beginning to wake up, 'I've got a nasty little red sore on my opisthenar.'

OPSIMATH *n.* One who learns late in life. From the Greek *opse* (late) and *manthano* (learn). Useful when writing out report cards. 'Timothy's results in English, History, Mathematics, Geography, Science, Physical Education, and Effort were, admittedly, a little disappointing, even for him; but at this stage he certainly has all the necessary grounding to seek to make a future for himself as an opsimath.'

OSCITATION *n.* Inattention; an overt display of lack of interest, with much yawning, etc. 'Go ahead,' you say encouragingly to the *aporial macrologist* (q.v.), 'I'm all oscitation!'

OTIOSE *a.* Serving no useful purpose. Alternatively: leisurely. Both meanings presumably come from the same Latin origin, *otium* (leisure) – in the former case no doubt via the intermediate concept of *idle*. The overtones of *odious, adipose*, and *obese* make this a useful word for unsettling the ignorant in casual conversation.

OUBLIETTE *n.* A dungeon, often in the form of a deep and narrow well, designed for the permanent incarceration of those whom it is desired to forget. From the French *oublier* (to forget). 'Out of sight, out of mind,' no doubt our medieval forebears (or at least those of them who owned castles) thought as the duke's tax-collector was lowered down the stone tube and the heavy iron lid clanged shut far above him. To modern ears, the word is not unsuggestive of some delicate item of Parisian millinery. 'Ah, I can just see you in a lovely little oubliette,' you rhapsodize to your sister when she finally emerges, fully made up, from the bathroom.

OXYMORON *n.* Extremely concise contradiction in terms, e.g., 'cruel kindness,' 'beloved enemy,' 'delicious sauerkraut.' One of those wonderfully named figures of speech that we all learnt about at school. (Remember metonymy? synecdoche?) It would be unreasonable to expect even the Superior Person to maintain a working knowledge of all these terms. The author suggests that one only be selected for memorizing and repeated use; his own favorite is aposiopesis, which he once used to great effect at a dog-poisoner's biennial, when – but that is another story.

P

PALIMPSEST *n.* A manuscript whose original writing has been scraped off or treated in some way so that a second layer of writing can be superimposed on the document. When your sister's new friend, the budding poet, shyly seeks your comment on his latest effort, a free-form rhapsody on the coming of autumn, you read it, stare as though entranced into the distance for a half-minute, and then say slowly: 'You know, I think I see the basis for a marvelous palimpsest in this.'

PALINOIA *n.* The compulsive repetition of an act, over and over again, until it is performed perfectly. One of the classic forms of the condition is of course the dogged piano practice of the freckled ten-year-old next door who is preparing the infamous Minute Waltz for the local eisteddfod. The technical term for this is pianola palinoia, and the condition brought on in the listener is known as pianola palinoia paranoia. To be preferred is palinoiac *paraphilemia* (q.v.).

PANDICULATION *n.* Stretching and yawning. 'This morning, right in the middle of my *ante-jentacular* [q.v.] pandiculation, ...'

PAPULIFEROUS *n.* Pimply. Typical condition of a *groak* (q.v.).

PARADIGM *n.* Model, pattern, or example. A pretentious and unnecessary word, normally found only in psychology theses. Never use this word yourself, but be prepared, when it is used by another, to lean forward intently, narrow your eyes, and say, 'Just a moment – do you really *mean* "paradigm" in *that* context?' When, somewhat bemused, he avers that he does, you merely raise your eyebrows and remain silent. With any luck at all, he will now have forgotten what he was going to say. Apply the same technique when confronted with *parameter, infrastructure, structure,* or *matrix* (q.v.).

PARALOGISM *n.* Illogical reasoning, the illogicality of which the reasoner in question is unaware of. 'Ah, Herr Doktor, how can I possibly hope to match you in paralogism?'

PARAMOUR *n.* Illicit lover. A rather beautiful word (from the French *par amour*, fairly obviously) which has undeservedly acquired a denigratory signification. Even the good Dr. Johnson seems to have regretted this, referring to it gratuitously as 'not inelegant or unmusical.'

PARAPHILEMIA *n.* Love play. When engaging a secretary, you tactfully ask each candidate at the interview whether she has suffered from any major medical problems; in the course of this you inquire gently: 'No paraphilemiaphobia, I hope?' She smiles blankly and shakes her head.

PARISOLOGY *n.* The deliberate pursuit of ambiguity in one's use of language. Like *charientism* (q.v.), an end to which this book is a means.

PARONOMASIA *n.* Wordplay of the punning kind, i.e., using similar-sounding (or identical-sounding) words with different meanings in close proximity to each other, for an effect of comedy, balance, or cleverness. *Paronomasiac* is an appropriate grandiloquism for punster, as well as for anyone with a penchant for messing around with words.

PARTURITION *n.* Childbirth. For referring to bodily functions, there is a range of Latinate expressions which are uncommon enough to lend interest to your discourse without being so outlandish as to convict you of preciosity. Also recommended are *gravid* and *enceinte* (both to be preferred to *pregnant*), and *micturition*.

PASTIME *n.* Game, recreation. Derived, believe it or not, from *pass* and *time*. Every schoolboy knows of the French sundial inscribed on one side *L'amour fait passer le temps* and on the other *Le temps fait passer l'amour*.

PEDAGOGY *n.* The science or art of teaching. Note that this is not a synonym for *teaching*; but, surprisingly, *pedagogue* indeed *is* a synonym for *teacher*. The word *pedagogue* is of some interest, in that its usage in England tends to be somewhat *pejorative* (q.v.) in *contradistinction* (q.v.) to its usage in French, there being connotations of pedantry in the English usage. The original derivation is from an Ancient Greek term describing a slave who led his master's children to school. The modern-day teacher is, of course, the slave of the children, but may be allowed to lead them to a local cinema for the afternoon as part of an elective course in media appreciation.

PEDICULAR *a.* Lousy. The pronunciation is almost identical with that of *particular*. Hence (to your sister, after she has refused to let you use her electric shaver): 'I didn't know you were quite so pedicular.'

PEEN *n.* The wedge-shaped or thin end of a hammer head. A ridiculous word. (See also *garb*.)

PEJORATIVE *a.* Derogatory. Often describing the use in this manner of a particular word or phrase not in itself necessarily derogatory, and – just to make this definition harder to follow – often used in the context of an assurance that the word or phrase in question is *not* being used in its derogatory sense, e.g., 'His approach was Machiavellian – I do not use the term in its pejorative sense.' This is the example *par excellence* of a Superior Word. The author has encountered few people who use it freely in normal conversation, but it is a word that the listener knows he has seen somewhere, knows he is not quite clear about, but feels he ought to be. For maximum effect it should be used glibly and casually, without special emphasis.

PERADVENTURE *adv.* The Superior alternative to *perhaps*.

PERNOCTATION *n.* In ecclesiastical usage, an all-night vigil. Literally, 'passing the night.' *Compernoctation* could thus be a useful neologism for 'spending the night together.'

PETARD *n.* Small explosive device, used by military engineers in medieval times to undermine castle walls, break down drawbridges, etc. 'It is now rarely used,' says Webster, rather sweetly. From the French *peter* (to break wind). The man who knows his Onions (the Shakespeare glossarist – *Ed.*) will be familiar with the use in *Hamlet*, Act III, Scene 4 – 'For 'tis the sport to have the engineer/Hoist with his own petard.'

PETTITOES *n.* Pig's trotters. According to Johnson, used by Shakespeare as a contemptuous term for feet; but not so recorded in Onions. 'Ah, Samantha, you have the sweetest little pettitoes.'

PIERIA *n.* A place in Thessaly, famed in legend as the location of the Pierian Spring, the fount of learning and poetry. Thus, from Pope's *Essay on Criticism*:

> 'A little learning is a dangerous thing;
> Drink deep, or taste not the Pierian Spring:
> There shallow draughts intoxicate the brain,
> And drinking largely sobers us again.'

The Superior Person should never quote a familiar maxim, such as the first line of the above, on its own – he should always quote the full context as well.

Another useful way to give this word an airing is to say to your cousin Ralph, as he leaves for home after an interminable weekend: 'By the way, I see that you're still free from any signs of Pieria.' He leaves in faint bemusement, under the impression that you have congratulated him on his dental health.

PIGSNEY *n.* Believe it or not, a term of endearment used when addressing a girl. From the Saxon word for girl. Try it out on your inamorata; she will surely be charmed and delighted. 'Come, my little pigsney ...'

PILGARLIC *n.* A poor, wretched, bald-headed man who presents a sorry spectacle. From *pilled* (peeled) garlic.

PLAUSIBLE *a.* Seemingly reasonable; convincing on the surface, but ... The word can be applied either to a statement or a person, as can its near-synonym *specious*; the marginal difference between the two words consists in the fact that *plausible* tends to be applied more naturally to persons, and *specious* to statements. The Concise Oxford Dictionary's definition of *plausible*, as applied to persons, reads in its entirety: '(of persons), fair-spoken (usually implying deceit).' What a world of disillusionment is embodied in those few words, torn as they seem to be from the soul of some careworn Oxonian lexicographer who sipped the wine of life and found it bitter.

PLENILUNARY *a.* Pertaining to the full moon. Useful for excuses. 'I'm awfully sorry, Cynthia – we'd love to come around tonight, but it's that time of the month again, I'm afraid, and we have to consider poor Quentin's plenilunary condition.'

PLETHORA *n.* Too many of a good or bad thing (cf. *surfeit*, too much of a good thing). The number of objects constituting a plethora varies. To the house-proud matron, a single cockroach in her kitchen is a plethora, since cockroaches are, to her, *anathema* (q.v.). Indeed, a house-proud matron is, by definition, someone with a plethora of anathemas.

POETASTER *n.* Ersatz and amateurish poet. The classic example in recent times was probably that of Simon Quinsy (see his biography, *Lank, Dank and Disgusting to Know*, by his lifetime friend and colleague the Hon. Roddie Smoothe-Lewis), whose heavily alliterative and strongly accented style, with its sudden descents from romance into realism, concealed what was seen even by his admirers as being, essentially, a total lack of meaning. All these features can be discerned in the following excerpt from the song cycle *Ear, Nose and Throat Ward*, on which he was working when he was first struck down by the appalling disease that was ultimately to take his life:

> 'O my marmoreal month of May,
> Twice-twisting, trembling in my tree,
> When will you wend your way away,
> At dismal dawning, or at about twenty-five
> past three?'

In connection with the second line of the above, it is perhaps worthy of mention that both Quinsy and Smoothe-Lewis pronounced *r* as *w* – a trait inherited by Quinsy and probably passed on to Smoothe-Lewis during their collaboration on the ill-fated comedy version of *Sartor Resartus*.

POPINJAY *n.* Empty-headed and pushy young *coxcomb* (q.v.). The emphasis here is on the brashness rather than the empty-headedness, and the image conveyed is of a garishly clad, interfering jabberer. The word is said to have originally described a target in the form of a parrot on a pole. Note the similarity to Papageno. One cannot help wondering who first had an idea so bizarre as that of using a parrot on a pole as a target. How, for that matter, was the parrot fixed to the pole? What did the parrot think of it? What, above all, was it a target for?

PRAGMATISM *n.* Mere expediency and low cunning. Formerly, a philosophical system adopted by a group of benevolent and forward-looking social reformers as the underpinning of their program for the enlightenment and advancement of society through educational processes that were creative, spontaneous, and equated the true with the good. *Sic transit gloria mundi.* An even earlier meaning of *pragmatical* (the common form of the adjective in the eighteenth century) was 'interfering and busybody-ish.' *Pragmaticalness* was, according to Johnson, 'the quality of intermeddling without right or call.'

PROCACITY *n.* Petulance; impudence. Not to be confused with *precocity*. 'I think Natalie shows very considerable procacity,' you say earnestly to Mrs. Eastwacker after her narcissistic daughter has just beaten your own in the eisteddfod elocution finals.

PROCELLOUS *a.* Stormy, tempestuous. 'What sort of a mood is he in?' you are asked by the next candidate as you part from the official tester after your driver's license test. 'Procellous, distinctly procellous,' you reply, with a reassuring smile.

PROCERITY *n.* Tallness, height. 'I think you showed great procerity out there, darling,' you say proudly to your gangling teenager after she has just done her bit in the ballet class's end-of-term performance.

PROLEGOMENA *n.* Introductory remarks, preliminary discussion. Much better than just saying *preface* or *prologue*.

PUSILLANIMITY *n.* Faint-heartedness. (Note that this is not quite a synonym for *cowardice*.) Much used by Dr. Johnson in the eighteenth century, and in the twentieth by a learned *clerical* (q.v.) gentleman of the author's acquaintance, who is given to remarking on 'the difficulty of drawing the line between Christian meekness and pusillanimity.' This is the kind of remark which, suitable though it is for the Superior Person, should be used only once in a lifetime. Its repetition entails the risk of a repeated hearing by the same individual, with a consequent diminution of lexical credibility on the part of the speaker.

Q

QUACKSALVER *n.* Much to be preferred to the more usual, abbreviated form *quack*: an ignorant pretender to medical skills. A quacksalver was one who quacked, or chattered boastfully, about his salves, or healing ointments. The abbreviated form is fairly commonly used nowadays by the disrespectful as a synonym for *doctor*, for reasons unknown to the author. The use in such instances of the full form of the word would, it is suggested, help to avoid embarrassment in the event of its inadvertent use in the presence of one of the medical fraternity; indeed, a casual reference to one's quacksalver may well pass unchallenged in a roomful of doctors, who will probably assume that you are speaking of an item of domestic silver.

QUADRAGENARIAN *n.* Someone who is between forty and fifty years of age. Since the word sounds to the uninitiated as though it means simply 'forty-year-old,' it is particularly suitable for use by forty-nine-year-olds as a self-descriptive.

QUAKEBUTTOCK *n.* A nicely scornful word for a coward.

QUALM *n.* A sudden uneasiness, generally about some action or proposed action of one's own. Less intellectual and more intuitive than a *scruple* (q.v.) or a misgiving. In modern parlance, the degree of uneasiness implied is only moderate, but formerly the use of the term implied nausea or even pain. The present meaning lies rather beautifully midway between those of *queasy* and *calm*, but the apparently hybrid spelling is purely fortuitous and has nothing to do with either word. Normally one has qualms rather than a qualm. 'I must confess to having some qualms about our new advertising slogan, Fosdyke.' But in such a case, exactly how many qualms does the speaker have? The author believes he has the answer to this. He has always seen a qualm as being a small, round, jellylike object about five centimeters in diameter – i.e., a pocket-sized object. The number of qualms normally held about anything would therefore equate to the number of pockets in a man's suit; that is, about half a dozen. This theory also fits the observed fact that women generally have fewer qualms than men.

QUAQUAVERSAL *a.* Pointing or facing in every direction. In relation to rock formations, the term specifically means sloping down in every direction from a more or less central tip. You might so refer to your Uncle Enderby's cranial structure.

QUEER PLUNGERS *n.* Not a reference to the lubricious doings of androgynes; a queer plunger was a rather charming form of eighteenth-century con man or confidence trickster. The following definition comes from Grose's *Dictionary of the Vulgar Tongue*: 'Cheats who throw themselves into the water, in order that they may be taken up by their accomplices, who carry them to one of the houses appointed by the Humane Society for the recovery of drowned persons, where they are rewarded by the Society with a guinea each; and the supposed drowned person, pretending he was driven to that extremity by great necessity, is also frequently sent away with a contribution in his pocket.'

QUERIMONY *n.* Complaint. *Querimonious* is a synonym of *querulous*, but the former is to be preferred on account of its superior grandiloquence. Should one of your immediate family be in the habit of having regular faultfinding sessions on your personal appearance, your clothes, your manners, your habits, etc., you might find an opportunity to refer to such sessions as his or her *quotidian* (q.v.) querimony ceremony.

QUIDDITY *n.* (i) The essence of something; literally, its *whatness*; (ii) a quibble, or trifling nicety. One might say that the quiddity of a quiddity is its quirkish, quizzical, quibbling quaintness.

QUIDNUNC *n.* A gossip; a stickybeak; one who is forever anxious to know about everything that is going on. Literally, 'what now?' Interestingly, the term was for a time more commonly taken to mean a politician. Grose mentions a character named Quidnunc, a politician, in a farce called *The Upholsterer*.

117

QUIESCENT *a.* At rest for the time being; dormant; in-active. The odd thing about this word is not what it means but what it does not mean. *Quiesce* means 'to grow quiet or still' and by any normal process *quiescent* should mean 'growing quiet or still'; instead, it has a quite specific usage, referring as it does always to a condition that was formerly active, is now in-active, but will become active again in due course – such as the reader's *cardialgia* (q.v.), or his wife's *oniomania* (q.v.).

QUIM *n.* The private parts of a woman (an eighteenth-century usage, possibly derived from *queme*, an obsolete word meaning 'pleasant, snug'). 'Ah, women,' you muse out loud, in the middle of your sister's bridal shower. 'I love them, for all their quims and fancies.' Alternatively, when you come upon your beloved apparently lost in reverie, you cry jovially: 'A *merkin* [q.v.] for your quim, my dear!' She assumes you to be using an esoteric variant of 'a penny for your thoughts,' and opens her heart to you.

QUISQUOUS *a.* Perplexing, puzzling. 'How extremely quisquous!' you declare, as you pore over the chessboard.

QUODLIBET *n.* (i) A debating point; a nice point, or scholastic subtlety raised for disputation. One might almost say that the *quiddity* (q.v.) of quodlibet is the same as the quiddity of a quiddity. (ii) An impromptu musical medley.

QUOTIDIAN *a.* Everyday; recurring daily; ordinary, commonplace. Can also be used as a noun, meaning a daily allowance or allotment. 'Have you had your quotidian yet?' is a question that will leave a friend nicely bemused. *Diurnal* in one of its senses means the same, but in another means 'by day,' as distinct from 'by night' – the opposite of *nocturnal*, in fact; hence it is not necessarily a solecism to speak of a diurnal quotidian. To speak of a nocturnal quotidian is, of course, quite another thing.

R

RAMPALLION *n.* A bold, forward, rampant, or wanton woman; a woman who romps. An Elizabethan term. Thus Falstaff to Mistress Quickly, when she attempts to have him arrested: 'Away, you scullion; you rampallion; you fustilarian! I'll tickle your catastrophe.' (*Henry IV Pt. II*, Act II, Scene 1.) A suggested modern use: 'Mom, can I have a rampallion for my birthday?' (Incidentally, a *fustilarian* is a fusty-lugs, or beastly, sluttish woman; and a *catastrophe*, in the above context, is a posterior.)

RANARIUM *n.* A frog farm. 'Better smarten up, Fosdyke, or it'll be the ranarium for you.'

RASORIAL *a.* Constantly scratching around in search of food, like a fowl (or a sister's boyfriend). Pronounced more or less in the same way as *risorial* (laughter-provoking) and *rosorial* (rodentlike; gnawing). 'I'm sorry if I sometimes seem ambivalent in my attitude to your mother, Natalie; it's just that I find it very hard to make up my mind whether I see her as essentially rasorial, rosorial, or risorial.'

REBARBATIVE *a.* Repulse, off-putting, daunting. A relatively innocuous-sounding epithet, and therefore suitable for use in relation to food, children, or dachshunds when in the presence of hostesses, mothers, and dog-owners.

RECIDIVISM *n.* Habitual relapsing into criminal or otherwise antisocial behavior. As, for example, a neighbor's habitually letting his German shepherd run loose in the street, playing Scott Joplin records at full volume, or assaulting itinerant Mormons. Note the difference from *atavism*, which is the reappearance of a more primitive form of behavior; as, for example, a neighbor running loose in the street himself, playing Scottish country dance records at full volume, or *not* assaulting itinerant Mormons.

RECREMENT *n.* A bodily secretion that is reabsorbed. The obvious example – indeed the only one known to the author, who is not, and does not seek to be, well-versed in such matters – is saliva. Rather than speak of a nubile damsel, or a plate of steaming frankfurters, as making your mouth water, you could refer to yourself as experiencing an increment in your recrement.

RECUSANT *n.* Refusing staunchly to comply with some generally accepted rule or custom. The most appropriate modern application would be to that small but hardy band who refuse to be searched, labeled, unlabeled, interrogated, or otherwise bullied or humiliated on their entrance to, or egress from, supermarket-style chain stores. 'Leave me alone!' they cry in ringing tones, on being approached by the store security officers; 'Go away! Stop bothering me, you rude man!' The author, whose natural *pusillanimity* (q.v.) prevents him from being more than a recusant *manqué* (q.v.), bows before them in respect and admiration.

REDIVIVUS *a.* Restored to life, or to full liveliness. Use *after* the noun, and preferably after an incongruously non-classical noun. If, for example, your name is Boggins, you might emerge from your shower, taken after a hard day's gardening, and cry to your wife: 'Behold! Boggins redivivus!'

REJECTAMENTA *n.* Things that have been rejected, as being worthless. A delicate way for a young lady to refer to a former suitor – 'one of my rejectamenta.'

REMARKS, EXASPERATING *n.* (See also *bully for you!* and *stout fellow!*) '*You are very wise.*' This is recommended as an effective all-purpose response on any occasion when you have been out-argued, ridiculed, shouted down, or simply proved hopelessly wrong. It should be uttered in a quiet, dignified fashion and with an earnest facial expression. Its effect is multiplied if it can be used again within the ensuing few minutes.

'*You may well be right.*' For use in similar circumstances to the above. Should be used, however, with studied nonchalance and a gentle smile, as though you have decided that the other party will have to be humored.

'*Spare me your rapierlike wit.*' For use when a spouse or workmate has made a successful sally at your expense. A little touch of mock supplication in your tone will help with this one.

'... *for want of a better word*.' Use immediately following any exceptionally grandiloquent or esoteric term. 'You don't find Gilbert to be a little ... er ... *ultracrepidarian* [q.v.] – for want of a better word?'

REMIPED *n.* Having feet that are adapted for use as oars. May be of use as a substitute for *megapod* (q.v.) when in the presence of a policeman.

REPULLULATE *v.* To sprout again; to recur, as a disease. The perfect verb with which to describe the reappearances of your beloved's young brother at the living-room door while you are engaged in an affectionate tête-à-tête with the young lady.

RESIPISCENCE *n.* Recognizing one's own error, or errors; seeing reason once again. 'I'm sure all of us look forward to your ultimate resipiscence, Jeremy.'

RHINOCEROTIC *a.* According to the author's sources, this means 'pertaining to rhinoceroses'; but, since *rhinal* means 'of the nose' (see *dirhinous*), he cherishes the thought that an equally valid meaning would be 'using the nose, or nostrils, for erotic purposes.'

RICTAL BRISTLE *n.* A feather resembling a bristle which grows from the base of a bird's bill. A rather sweet name for your sister's boyfriend's incipient beard.

RICTUS *n.* A fixed gaping of the mouth, or grinning. *Rictus sardonicus* is the fixed grin on the face of one who has just died from strychnine poisoning, which induces muscular contractions; *rictus politicus*, that on the face of a Congressman who has just been confronted on live television with the news that he has lost his seat as a result of an unexpected swing during late counting of votes on election night; and *rictus excruciatus*, that on the face of the author when he suddenly realizes that he has forgotten the names of *both* of the two people whom he is trying to introduce to each other.

RODOMONTADE *n.* Empty boasting and blustering; arrogant ranting, braggadocio. From Rodomont, a Moorish hero in Ariosto's *Orlando Furioso*. The nearest thing to a modern example that springs to mind is the televised prating of professional wrestlers, boxers, and politicians; but in at least two of these three cases there is an underlying suggestion of self-awareness and good humor that prevents the term being fully applicable. Note, incidentally, that *braggadocio* can be either the language that is spoken or the person who speaks it.

RONION *n.* A term of abuse for a woman, found in Shakespeare (*Merry Wives of Windsor* and *Macbeth*). The meaning is not entirely clear: Webster relates it to the French *rogne* (scab or mange) and suggests 'scabby, mangy'; but Johnson, more convincingly in view of Shakespeare's 'rump-fed ronyon,' relates it to the French *rognon* (the loins) and suggests 'fat, bulky.'

RUGOSE *a.* Corrugated with wrinkles. 'Ah, Mrs. Sandalbath, there must be many a woman half your age with a complexion not nearly as rugose as yours.'

S

SAL VOLATILE *n.* Understood by the author to be the name of a young American film-star, of southern European descent, who made his name in the fifties doing bit parts in rock 'n' roll movies.

SAPID *a.* Flavorsome, lively, interesting. The opposite of *vapid*, and of *insipid*, but vaguely suggestive of both words and hence ideal for the Compliment Reluctant: 'I'm so glad you've invited Charles; I always find his conversation so sapid.' Or the Insult Apparent: 'So Charles is coming, eh? Hmmm ... do you think he'll fit in? His conversation is always so ... sapid.'

SAPONACEOUS *a.* Soapy. Though the word comes from the objective realms of scientific and technological terminology, it could equally well be used metaphorically, in the sense of 'unctuous,' 'greasily ingratiating,' or 'Uriah Heepish.'

SAPOROUS *a.* Tasty, flavorsome. Like *saponaceous*, an objective scientific term that calls out for a more colorful usage. On being introduced to the couple who clearly regard themselves as two of the Beautiful People and who have just made their Impressive and Well-Timed Entrance, you exclaim admiringly: 'Ah, how perfect! The marriage of the saponaceous and the saporous!' Their evening is tormented by the necessity to remember the two words until they can get home and look them up in the dictionary; and when they do, they find themselves plagued by uncertainty as to which term you were applying to which person.

SARCOPHAGOUS *a.* No, not the stone coffin from which a muslin-swathed Lon Chaney practices *anabiosis* (q.v.), hand-first, to the dismay of a nearby Nubian or nubile. That is spelled *sarcophagus*, without the second *o*. The former word means flesh-eating, or carnivorous. Actually, the latter word is basically the same, despite its *o*-less condition, since it was originally a coffin used by the ancient Greeks which, because of the particular kind of limestone of which it was made, did in fact consume the corpse, i.e., eat flesh. If you are a vegetarian, you might refer to your meat-eating acquaintances as sarcophagous.

SATRAP *n.* A petty or subordinate ruler with despotic powers within his own realm. An assistant principal, bus driver, dental nurse, head of a typing pool, hospital matron, motor-vehicle inspector, or headwaiter.

SCIOLISM *n.* Superficial knowledge; a show of learning without any substantial foundation. 'As always, Herr Doktor, I bow to your superior sciolism.'

128

SCRUPLE *n.* The common meaning, of course, is a feeling of reluctance or a hesitation, based on conscientious concern for a principle. In this sense, the word evokes conjecture about the precise number and nature of the scruples held in a particular instance. (See also *qualm.*) Whereas the author envisages a qualm as a small jellylike object carried in the pocket, he has always envisaged a scruple as being a small purple pretzel-shaped object caught in the hair. This also helps to account for the observed fact that women have more scruples than men. (See, again, *qualm.*) Be that as it may, there is a secondary (originally the primary) meaning for *scruple*: an extremely small unit of weight. This enables you to liven up a moribund party by declaring, during a quiet moment, that you know for a fact, and can prove, that Arabella has fewer scruples than Felicity.

SELF-ACTUALIZATION *n.* Self-realization. A term invented by contemporary educational theorists who envisage the liberated child opening like a flower before them as his natural instincts unfold and his own special talents and personality traits emerge and develop to their full in a free and open environment, untrammeled by outside interference. It is difficult to point to particular examples of the process in operation; but the life of Heinrich Himmler, or the growth of a cauliflower, appear to the author to fit the terms of the theory.

SEMPITERNAL *a.* The Superior Person's word for *eternal.* Strictly speaking, a somewhat tautological construction, deriving as it does from the Latin *semper* (always) and *aeternus* (eternal); but pleasingly archaic and rhetorical in flavor. Slightly confusing to the listener also: if your wife overhears you declaring a sempiternal affection for your secretary, you can always explain that the word you were using was *semi-paternal*.

SERMOCINATION *n.* The practice of making speeches; the habit of preaching constantly. (See *stentorophonic*.)

SESQUIPEDALIAN *a.* Inordinately long (of words). Literally, a foot and a half long – hence, a word of that length. As a noun: an inveterate user of such words; a practitioner of the lore contained in this book; a *word-grubber* (q.v.).

SEXIST *a.* Tacitly assuming a conventional set of differences between the sexes. Not, as might appear at first sight, an active practitioner of sexual behavior.

SHANDYGAFF *n.* The full and proper name for what most people call a shandy. In the future, *never* use the abbreviated version; always the full. Know, too, that a shandygaff is properly not beer and lemonade, but beer and ginger beer. A young lady should always insist on the proprieties being observed in these matters.

SHIBBOLETH *n.* A doctrine or principle once held essential by a particular group or party but now seen as rather old-hat, if not abandoned altogether. It is probably a comment on the nature of life and mutability, rather than on etymological processes, that the original meaning was a password or other identifying sign, such as an opinion or style of dress, that distinguished the members of a particular group because of their unique attachment to it. Thus advocacy of the nationalization of industry was a shibboleth of the political left wing in former years in a sense quite different from that in which it is now their shibboleth. Just how important it was in earlier times to be on the right side of a shibboleth can be judged from the original usage in Judges 12: 5-6: '... and it was so, that when those Ephraimites which were escaped said, Let me go over; that the men of Gilead said unto him [*sic*], Art thou an Ephraimite? If he said, Nay; Then said they unto him, Say now Shibboleth: and he said Sibboleth: for he could not frame to pronounce it right. Then they took him, and slew him ...'

SHITTLECOCK *n.* The true, proper, and original form of *shuttlecock*, from the Old English *scytel*, or bolt. Apparently fallen into *desuetude* (q.v.) in this form since the eighteenth century, for reasons unknown to the author. Its use in the original form is to be preferred, especially when playing badminton with your sister. (See also *bumblepuppy.*)

SHOULDERCLAPPER *n.* A Shakespearean term (*Comedy of Errors*) meaning a person who 'affects familiarity' but at the same time 'mischiefs privily.' Included here to give the author the opportunity of quoting from Johnson's superb definition.

SIMPLETON *n.* A person of little brainpower. There is a suggestion, too, of well-meaningness and gullibility. 'A democratic franchise of one simpleton, one vote' (Shaw). The formation of the word by the addition to *simple* of *ton* (the latter perhaps an elision of 'the one'?) is pleasing, and suggests the similar formation of others, such as *feebleton, littleton,* etc. Grose suggests that *ton* is short for *Tony,* but gives no hint as to who the unfortunate Anthony, thus immortalized, may have been.

SLUBBERDEGULLION *n.* A glorious seventeenth-century term of contempt (found in *Hudibras*), apparently meaning a dirty, wretched slob.

SOLIPSIST *n.* A philosopher who holds that only he himself exists, and that the external world exists only through his own conception of it. It is amusing to consider the spectacle of two solipsists at a philosophy seminar suspiciously eyeing each other and wondering which one of them is a figment of the other's imagination. The author prefers to use this term to describe any extremely self-centered person – one who is so wrapped up in himself that he behaves as though the external world does in fact exist only insofar as it serves his purposes. Thus, you are reclining on the golden sands, savoring the warm sun, the salt-sea breeze, and the gentle murmuring of the waves; the person who sits down beside you and turns on a transistor radio, which is tuned to a talk show, is a solipsist. You reach the top of a crowded escalator in a busy department store; the person on the step above you who, on stepping off the moving stairs, immediately stops dead, stands stock still, and looks around in a leisurely fashion, is a solipsist.

SOMETIME *a.* Former. As in 'sometime lecturer in Multicultural Studies at the Royal Military College.' A delightful archaism. Ideal for use in addressing envelopes to easily embarrassable friends: 'Mr. J. Smith, Esq.,/Sometime Fellow in Ecclesiastical Parlance,/etc., etc.'

SPHRAGISTICS *n.* The study of engraved seals. The Superior Person should be equipped with as many such terms as possible so that he can make casual references to his familiarity with the most outré studies and pursuits. 'I remember, back in the days when I was reading sphragistics at Balliol, ...' In this case, though, even the author does admit to *qualms* (q.v.) about the pursuit in question. The studies themselves would seem inoffensive enough, but the cruelty, the inhumanity of the original engraving process ...

SPURIOUS *a.* Not genuine. This is not, however, simply a synonym for *fake*. The spurious have pretensions of a kind, but fall short of fulfilling them. 'The degree of accuracy implied in these statistics is spurious.' A lovely word to say aloud, flowing as it does off the tongue. Practice saying 'your prurience is spurious' – this could be a nicely ambivalent compliment for one of your friends.

STEATOPYGOUS *a.* Fat-buttocked. Another excellent word for insulting without offending, especially as the listener is unlikely to be able to remember it long enough to look it up in a dictionary later, and is unlikely in any case to possess a dictionary that includes it.

STENTOROPHONIC *a.* Speaking very loudly. From Stentor, the Greek herald in the Trojan war, whose voice, according to Homer, was as loud as that of fifty men combined. There is always at least one stentorophone in close proximity in any public gathering where you are trying to enjoy a quiet conversation with a friend. 'Do we *have* to invite Mr. Wangensteen this time? I mean, it's bad enough having someone who's *sermocinatious* [q.v.], but when they're stentorophonic as *well* ...'

STOUT FELLOW! *n.* Exclamation indicative not of abhorrence of perceived corpulence, but of friendly admiration for a worthy act or statement. Thus, *A*: 'I was caned by my teacher every time I talked out of turn, and I believe that made me the man I am today.' *B*: 'Stout fellow!' Or, *A*: 'I am not prepared to sit idly by while this government ruins the country's economy.' *B*: 'Stout fellow!' This usage derives from what was formerly the primary meaning of *stout* (brave or resolute). The modern meaning is, of course, plump or tending to fatness; a fact which permits a nice degree of innuendo in the use of the above expression when it is addressed to people who are, in fact, slightly overweight.

STRUCTURE *n.* Goering is debited with the oft-quoted: 'When I hear the word *culture*, I reach for my gun.' The author reacts in the same fashion to the indiscriminate use of the word *structure* to convey a range of half-formed and tenuous notions of an over-conceptualized nature, unrelated to constructional manner or form, the latter being the true sense of the word. *Structure* is *not* a synonym for words such as *theory, belief, argument,* or *concept.* The rule is simple: when the word is used in any sense other than that of its dictionary definition, interrupt the speaker immediately and say, 'What, precisely, do you mean by "structure" in this context?' After three such interruptions in the course of any one faculty soirée, you will either have been marked down as a future dean or politely invited to help with the canapés in the kitchen. The latter is, of course, the preferred alternative.

STUPEFYING *a.* Inducing stupor. As, for example, the music of Scott Joplin, or a televised golf tournament. If used in a sufficiently favorable tone of voice ('How positively stupefying!'), it can be successfully confused in the listener's mind with *stupendous*.

SUBAUDITION *n.* Not an audition for an understudy, but the act of reading between the lines or otherwise understanding a message that is implicit rather than explicit. Thus, when your beloved, speaking of something she has just cooked, sewn, knitted, or handicrafted, asks, 'Do you really like it, though? Tell me truly now – I want your honest opinion,' it is by an act of subaudition that you know that what she really means is: 'Tell me immediately that you like this very much; you may use superlatives if you wish, but please be convincing.'

SUBDERISORIOUS *a.* Mocking, but gently and with affection – as between friends or lovers. A needed word, describing as it does a particular quality for which there is no other satisfactory adjective. The attitude of the author's wife to his *nikhedonia* (q.v.) over the present book.

SUCCEDANEUM *n.* A substitute, resorted to when the real thing is not available. Normally an object (as, for instance, a baby's pacifier); but may be used of persons (as, for instance, by Walpole: 'In lieu of me, you will have a charming succedaneum, Lady Harriet Stanhope'). The latter is the model for the Superior Person to cultivate. The *cc* is pronounced *ks*, by the way; there is no feminine (or masculine) form; the plural is *succedanea*.

succedaneum

SUFFUMIGATE *v.* To subject to smoke and fumes, more especially from below. Suffumigation is the process to which you are subjected in an elevator by a short person smoking a pipe.

SUGGILATE *v.* To beat black and blue; to bruise. When approached in the street for the twenty-third time by a jovial enthusiast soliciting money for a religious organization, you say, with an apologetic smile, 'I'm awfully sorry – I can't manage a cash donation at this time; but I could offer a suggilation, if that would do instead.'

SUMPTUARY and **SUMPTUOUS** *a.* The latter's meaning of luxurious, splendid, costly is well enough known, but the former is less familiar. It means 'having to do with the regulation or control of expenditure.' As Trent and Tabitha proceed down the aisle, you exclaim: 'Ah! The marriage of the sumptuous with the sumptuary!' When tackled on the matter, however, you decline to say which is which.

SUPEREXCRESCENCE *n.* Something growing superfluously. 'Sir, allow me to inform you that you are superexcrescent.'

SUPPOSITIOUS and **SUPPOSITITIOUS** *a.* As in the case of *abnegate, abrogate,* etc., the problem here is in grasping and retaining the difference in meaning. The former means supposed, assumed, hypothetical, conceptual, or notional; the latter means *spurious* (q.v.), phony, bogus, or ersatz. If at all possible, try to use both words in the one sentence, with a *very* straight face: 'I don't think we should dismiss Simon's standpoint out of hand; it's not necessarily supposititious just because it's suppositious, you know.'

SUSURRANT *a.* Gently whispering and rustling. Precisely descriptive of the surface noise emanating from your old long-playing records – or your new ones when your two-year-old has, in your absence, turned the treble control all the way up.

SYMPOSIUM *n.* Discussion of a set subject by a group of people, each of whom makes a contribution. Common enough a word in this sense, but what is less commonly known is its original sense – a post-prandial drinking party, with dancers and music. Hence the usefulness of the word. 'Sorry to rush through dinner tonight, Mother; Ethel and I have to attend a symposium at eight o'clock.'

T

TATTERDEMALION *n.* A ragged person whose clothes are always in tatters. To be preferred to *ragamuffin*, the nearest to an equivalent, because much less common and also because of the more equivocal etymology and signification of the latter. *Ragamuffin* in modern use is a ragged young scapegrace – a rather likable fellow whose escapades have a certain panache and whose worst sins are untidiness and recklessness. Formerly, the term meant much the same as *tatterdemalion* does now, a muff or muffin being a wretched or sorry creature and a ragamuffin thus being a sorry wretch in rags. As in *Henry IV Pt. I,* Act V, Scene 3, where Falstaff says, on his escape from the battle: '... God keep lead out of me! I need no more weight than mine own bowels. I have led my ragamuffins where they are peppered: there's not three of my hundred and fifty left alive.' Going back further still, however, the word may have had a much stronger meaning, being in fact, according to Webster, the name of the demon Ragamoffyn.

TAXONOMY *n.* In biology, the systematic classification of all organisms. Taken over recently by the social sciences as a piece of cant terminology useful for impressing the layman and for lengthening the curriculum of teacher training courses. Thus, where formerly we might have had, in botany, a taxonomy of blooms, we now have Bloom's Taxonomy of Educational Objectives. By the same process, we may shortly be confronted with Sudd's Taxonomy of Ulterior Motives, Lindenblatt's Taxonomy of Unequivocal Statements, Simonson's Taxonomy of Snide Remarks, Ferrett's Taxonomy of Unexpected Reactions, Palethorpe's Taxonomy of Predictable Thesis Topics, Pelsart's Taxonomy of Inescapable Obligations, Runciman's Taxonomy of Buns, Wendelhead's Taxonomy of Impossible Dreams, d'Umbrella's Taxonomy of Foregone Conclusions, Friedlander's Taxonomy of Dubious Propositions, Bone's Taxonomy of Firm Criteria, Eiderdown's Taxonomy of Unfortunate Oversights, Bastable's Taxonomy of Political Campaign Tricks, Esterhazy's Taxonomy of Losing Poker Hands, Podder's Taxonomy of Missing Shopping Carts – and, of course, the present author's Taxonomy of Otiose Taxonomies.

TEMULENCY *n.* Inebriation, drunkenness. Another good one for sick-leave application forms.

TERATOSIS *n.* A biological freak, or monstrosity. Thence *teratism*, which means 'the adoration of the monstrous.' After your sister and her latest boyfriend have spent forty-three minutes on the telephone while you are waiting to use it, you remark admiringly upon the sheer extent of their mutual teratism.

TERGIVERSATE *v.* To equivocate; to change from one opinion to another repeatedly. 'Would you care to tergiversate over the menu now, dear?'

TETRAGRAM *n.* A word with four letters. Note that the phrase 'four-letter word' is *pejorative* (q.v.), but that *tetragram* is not. Do what you can to remedy this situation.

TETRAGRAMMATON *n.* The Hebrew word for God, written with the four letters *YHVH*. The ideal personalized number plate for the Superior Person's car.

THAUMATURGE *n.* A wonder-worker, miracle man, or magician. *Thaumaturgus* was a term applied by the medieval Catholic Church to some of its saints, such as Gregory, Bishop of Neo-Caesarea, and St. Bernard, who was known as Thaumaturgus of the West. From this usage the term seems to have gradually descended to include in its coverage any kind of wonder-worker, including a conjuror or practitioner of legerdemain (i.e., sleight of hand). The nearest modern equivalent to the original meaning would seem to be the road-service mechanics employed by motorists' organizations such as AAA and the like.

THELYPHTHORIC *a.* That which corrupts women. The author's sources do not, unfortunately, identify the object so described; if any reader has one, perhaps he would be kind enough to send it to the author, enclosed in a plain wrapper.

THEOMANIA *n.* A psychopathic condition in which the sufferer believes himself to be God. Clinical notes:

Before administering sedatives or group therapy to the patient, the prudent psychiatrist will first ensure, by applying an appropriate test, that the patient's fixation does not have a basis in fact. For this purpose, crucifixion is *contraindicated* (q.v.), since a delay of three days is necessary to confirm a positive result, and in the event of a negative result the patient's condition will be terminal.

THERMANASTHESIA *n.* Inability to feel heat and cold. The use of this term might justifiably be adapted to signify insensitivity to the one *or* the other. Each of us knows someone who may be found rejoicing, coatless, in the bracing early-morning air of a late winter's day; and each of us knows someone who may be found huddled over the radiator, shivering, on a balmy spring evening. Fate has decreed that the two invariably marry each other. The lexicographer's contribution to their plight is that they may henceforth excuse their own condition, or commiserate with their helpmeet's, by the use of the above term.

THURIFICATION *n.* The act of burning incense, or of filling a room with the fumes of burning incense. From the Latin *thus, thuris* (frankincense). *Thuriferous* means 'producing or carrying incense.' 'I'm afraid we'll have to call in the drug squad again, Principal; the air in the prefects' room is distinctly thuriferous.'

TITULAR *a.* Derived from the holding of a title; nominal. Thus the titular head of a country is usually the President, Prime Minister, Dictator, etc., as distinct from the effective head, who is usually his wife, cleaning lady, golfing partner, etc.

TOKENISM *n.* (i) The appointment of a female to a government committee; (ii) the appointment of a member of a minority group to a government committee. (See also *hypertokenism*.)

thermanasthesia

TREMELLOSE *a.* Shaking like jelly. 'Your lactifera are tremellose!' you call out across the paddock to your large cousin Matilda as she performs an act of equitation. She assumes you to be warning her that her stirrup-leathers are loose.

TRILEMMA *n.* A problem situation in which there are not two, as in a dilemma, but *three* possible courses of action, each having its own disadvantages. Didn't know about this one, did you? You will find it depressingly useful in many life situations, including negotiations with auto repair shops, marital arguments (see also *zugzwang*), real-estate transactions, maternal visits, children's birthday parties, domestic budgeting, etc.

TURDIFORM *a.* Like a thrush in shape, the thrush being a bird of the family Turdidae.

U

ULIGINOUS *a.* Growing in muddy, oozy, or swampy places. 'Hmm,' you comment, after looking into your young brother's bedroom, 'I see Clive is going through another of his uliginous phases.'

ULLAGE *n.* The amount by which a liquid falls short of filling its container – whether because of evaporation, leakage, or any other reason. 'Well, old chap, since you were kind enough to bring along a bottle of truly excellent wine, I think I owe it to you to make sure you get all the ullage.'

ULOTRICHOUS *a.* Having short curly or woolly hair. Included here to give the author an excuse for introducing the following time-honored conundrum.

Question: 'Where do girls have short curly hair?'

Answer: 'New Guinea.'

ultracrepidarian

ULTRACREPIDARIAN *a.* Going too far; overstepping the mark; presumptuous; intruding in someone else's business. 'Sir, you are an ultracrepidarian bounder.'

ULTRAMONTANE *a.* Beyond the mountains. Formerly, that faction within the Catholic Church which either lived north of the Alps, outside of Italy, and opposed the concept of papal supremacy, or lived south of the Alps, within Italy, and favored the concept of papal supremacy. Nowadays, more commonly used simply to mean situated beyond the mountains. As, for example, Palm Springs. Not to be confused with *ultramundane*, which means beyond the realities of earthly existence; unreal, unworldly. As, for example, Palm Springs. Not to be confused, also, with *ultra-mundane* (with a hyphen), which means excessively humdrum. As, for example, Palm Springs.

ULULATION *n.* A howling or wailing. The correct term for the sound of a discussion between a fully-grown female human and her mother-in-law on the subject of domestic management, occurring toward the end of a protracted visit by the latter to the former's place of residence.

UMBRIFEROUS *a.* Superior word for shady. 'Ah, my love,' you rhapsodize, 'let us retire to an umbriferous *dingle* [q.v.].'

UNBELIEVER'S DEFENSE, THE *phr.* A technique devised by the author to enable schoolchildren and military personnel to avoid scripture lessons and church functions if they wish. The method is not to profess agnosticism, Hinduism, Buddhism, Islam, or atheism – an approach fraught with incidental irritations – but to assert allegiance to a sect so little-known or so obsolete that it can safely be assumed that your school or regiment will not be able to provide the necessary specialist personnel for your pastoral care. Suggested as particularly suitable for this purpose are the following sects:

The Abecedarians, who claimed that, since knowledge of the scriptures was passed on by the Holy Spirit, it was wrong to learn to read. (Allegiance to this sect can have obvious advantages in the school situation.)

The Docetists, who believed that a mere phantom, not the real Jesus, was crucified.

The Monophysites, who believed that Christ's human and divine natures were one and the same.

The Muggletonians, who believed that the Father, not the Son, died on the cross, and that the Aaron of the Book of Revelation was Lodowick Muggleton, a seventeenth-century tailor.

The Nestorians, who believed that Mary should not be called the Mother of God, as she was the mother only of the human side, not of the divine side, of Jesus.

The Origenists, who believed that men's souls are created before their bodies.

The Quietists, who believed that man should occupy himself wholly with the continuous contemplation of God, to the point of becoming detached from influence by his senses or by the world around him. Especially suitable for use in the military world.

The Sabellists, who believed that God is indivisible but has three successive roles.

The Sandemanians or *Glassites*, who believed that justifying faith is no more than a simple assent to the divine testimony passively received by the understanding. Before you query the meaningfulness of this, know that Michael Faraday was one of their number.

The Southcottians, followers of Joanna Southcott, who announced when she was over fifty that she was about to give birth to a divine man named Siloh.

The Supralapsarians, who held that God put Man into a position which made it inevitable that he would sin, and that his Creator would thereby have the opportunity of redeeming or punishing him.

UNNUN *v.* To defrock (metaphorically speaking) a nun. A delightful word in itself, and a formidable Scrabble weapon to boot.

UNUNDULATING *a.* A pleasing neologism of the author's, meaning 'not undulating,' 'not wavelike in shape or motion,' i.e., flat. As for instance, 'the ununduulating plains.'

UROPYGIUM *n.* The fleshy and bony prominence at the

posterior end of a bird's body – the part of the bird to which its tail feathers are attached. Might be loosely used at the Christmas dinner table as a grandiloquism for the pope's nose. More loosely still, might be used in church as a cryptograndiloquism for the pope's nose.

USTULATE *a.* Scorched. The Superior Person's word for sunburned.

USUFRUCT *n.* The right of using, benefiting from, and otherwise enjoying the fruits or output of someone else's property without damaging or diminishing the property itself. From the Latin *usus* (use) and *fructus* (fruit). A truly luscious word, if somewhat formidable to pronounce (*you-zoo-frukt*, with the emphasis on the *you*). 'May I hold your daughter in usufruct for the evening, Mrs. Galbally?'

UVULA *n.* The inverted cone of flesh hanging down from the soft palate at the back of the mouth. If your little soirée is being overwhelmed by the continuous neighing and trumpeting of the society matron brought along by your cousin Timothy, the interior decorator, you should quietly sidle up to her and, with conspiratorial confidentiality, whisper in her ear: 'I thought I should tell you – your uvula's showing.' At best, she can be expected to leave at once with Timothy; at next best, without him; and at worst, to spend at least twenty minutes locked in the bathroom examining her person in minute detail.

UXORILOCAL *a.* Living with one's wife's family. A suitable benison for a bride: 'May your husband be ever *uxorious* [q.v.] and never uxorilocal.' For a suitable curse, transpose the adjectives.

UXORIOUS *a.* Overly fond of a wife. The Concise Oxford Dictionary defines the meaning as 'excessively fond of one's wife'; but there does not appear to be anything in the etymology which excludes from the term's coverage the wives of others. However, if the conventional meaning is accepted, then, when next you are a wedding guest (and if you are a practicing exponent of the lore contained in this book, you had better make the most of it, since it may be the last time you are a guest anywhere), you quietly take the bride to one side, just before the happy couple is about to depart, and say to her: 'Jennifer, there's something you ought to know about Cyril. It's only fair to prepare you in advance for this. The fact is that you will find him extremely uxorious. I only hope ...' (At this point you break away as if you have seen someone approaching and must on no account be overheard.)

V

VAPULATION *n.* Flogging. Widespread ignorance of this word makes its use ('By God, old boy, I believe you deserve a vapulation for that!') quite safe even when addressing a Professor of English Language and Literature.

VARLET *n.* Low, menial scoundrel. One of a number of words of medieval origin, all indicative of unsavory status. Presumably the relatively large number of such words in existence is a reflection of the relatively high incidence of unsavoriness during the Middle Ages. Others that spring to mind are *lackey* (obsequious and servile hanger-on); *knave* (low-class rogue); and *caitiff* (base, despicable person). Note that knaves are always scurvy, i.e., thoroughly nasty, as is the appearance of one suffering from scurvy, one of the symptoms of which is scurf, or flaking skin, one of the instances of which is dandruff. Scurvy is a good descriptive for varlets, too, but not for lackeys. *Vassals* are also lowly creatures, but not as necessarily disreputable as varlets, lackeys, knaves, and caitiffs.

VECORDIOUS *a.* Mad, obsessive, senseless. The noun is *vecordy*. The general sense of the term is one of folly and dotage rather than of insanity. Useful for the Insult Concealed, especially in relation to the foibles of pet-fanciers, fishermen, golfers, stamp collectors, car-lovers, audio fanatics, sunbathers, lexicographers, train-spotters, bird watchers, joggers, oenologists, pedestrians, vegetarians, marching girls, film buffs, environmentalists, bibliophiles, mountaineers, *et hoc genus omne.*

velleity

VELLEITY *n.* A gentle volition; an almost passive inclination toward some act or objective. 'I sense within myself a certain velleity to get up and go to work,' you murmur to your semi-dormant helpmeet at eight A.M., as the sunlight creeps slowly across the *counterpane* (q.v.).

VELLICATE *v.* Twitch; or cause to twitch. 'There's no need for all that vellication, Nathan; Mother doesn't come here very often, and it's the only chance she gets to listen to all her Scottish country dance records on a really good stereo system.'

VELOCIPEDE *n.* A light vehicle propelled by the rider – strictly speaking, by the rider's feet. A genuinely useful word, since it covers not only bicycles but also tricycles, dinkies, toy cars, scooters, and the author's VW. When your cul-de-sac is replete with preschoolers and their older siblings, all pedaling away, circling and recircling the macadam like so many cruising sharks, you may properly refer to the scene as exhibiting a *plethora* (q.v.) of velocipedes.

VENEFICIAL *a.* (i) Acting by poison, or poisoning; (ii) acting by, or used in, witchcraft or sorcery, as for instance a witches' brew; (iii) relating to the doings of Venus, the goddess of love. The three meanings come together when your beloved cooks you a meal for the first time. The word is almost indistinguishable from *beneficial* if used casually in conversation.

VENERATION *n.* Profound respect and reverence. From the same root, ultimately, as *venereal* (i.e., pertaining to Venus). A piquant compliment to pay to an attractive member of the opposite sex is: 'Sir/Madam, you excite my veneration.'

VENERY *n.* (i) Sexual indulgence; (ii) hunting. A perfectly ambiguous word. While dining with a former duck-shooting companion and his wife, you could lean toward the latter during a break in the conversation and quietly ask: 'And is Athol still getting as much fun as he used to out of all that venery he went in for?'

VERACIOUS *a.* Of a truthful disposition. Pronounced exactly the same as *voracious*, i.e., of a greedy disposition. (See *ataxy.*)

VIOL *n.* Medieval six-stringed instrument; the predecessor of the violin, viola, and cello. Note that the viola is not a large violin; the violin is simply a small viola, since the word *violin* comes from *violino* (Italian, diminutive of *viola*). Note also that the cello is not a large viola; the proper term, which should *always* be used in its full form, is *violoncello* (n.b., *not* violincello), also from the Italian, being the diminutive of *violone*, or large viol. Got that?

VIRAGO *n.* A fierce, bad-tempered woman; a termagant. The derivation is from *vir* (a man). A virago is thus a mannish woman. The implication that being mannish is tantamount to being bad-tempered and violent seems to the author to be grossly discriminatory against his sex; he recommends, therefore, as the preferred expression, the virtual synonym *termagant*. The latter's derivation is much more fun. Oddly enough, it originally applied to men, not women. The term appears to have descended from *Tirmagian*, a Persian lord or god. The Crusaders apparently confused his followers with their enemies the Moslems, and this led in turn to *Termagant* becoming a stock figure on the medieval stage – a shouting, brawling, clubbing villain. (See *Hamlet,* Act III, Scene 2 – 'I could have such a fellow whipped for o'erdoing Termagant.') The transition of this figure into a stereotype of the brawling female is thought to be due to the fact that Termagant was traditionally represented on the stage in Eastern robes, like those worn in Europe by women.

VIRGINAL *n.* A small spinet without legs – a musical instrument used in Tudor and Elizabethan times.

When next you call in at your neighborhood music store, choose the shop assistant who looks as though he/she knows least about music (this will not be easy – the competition will be pretty fierce); approach him or her with apparent diffidence, looking shiftily from side to side; cough quietly and say: 'Ah, excuse me – ah, I wonder if I might have – I don't see it on the shelves – ah, perhaps you have it under the counter – ah, a copy of the, er ...' (Here you cough again, lean over the counter, and whisper), '... Fitzwilliam Virginal Book?'

VOUCHSAFE *v.* Deign to grant or offer. Literally, to guarantee, or vouch for the security of. Appropriately used in reference to such acts as giving your son his pocket-money, or his providing his services for thirty minutes' work in the garden. Should, if at all possible, be used in the same sentence as *eschew* (avoid, abstain from). Thus: 'Darling, if you could see your way clear to vouchsafe me the use of the car tomorrow, I think I can undertake to eschew any reference to the dents in the fender.'

W

WEDBEDRIP *n.* An agreement under which a feudal lord's tenant was bound to provide him, on request, with a day's reaping from the tenant's land. Instead of telling your workmates on Friday that you will be spending the weekend gardening, you could say that you have to carry out wedbedrip for your wife.

WHIPPERSNAPPER *n.* Intrusive young upstart. Someone younger, pushier, and callower than the author. Interesting that it is almost invariably preceded by the adjective *young*, even though the notion of youth is intrinsic to the noun itself. (See *codger.*)

WINCHESTER GOOSE *n.* This Elizabethan euphemism means a swelling in the groin caused by venereal disease. It seems to have been a favorite with Shakespeare, who used it at least twice (*King Henry VI Pt. I,* and *Troilus and Cressida*). The interest is in the derivation, the expression having arisen from the fact that the brothels of Southwark were under the jurisdiction of the Bishop of Winchester. As your dinner companions *tergiversate* (q.v.) over the menu and the waiter becomes more and more unhelpful, you say to your escort: 'I wonder if these are all the poultry dishes they have – ask him if he has Winchester goose.' You then retire quickly to the powder room to avoid the ensuing confusion.

WITHERSHINS or **WIDDERSHINS** *adv.* In an unfortunate direction. From the Middle High German *wider* (against) and *sin* (direction). In particular, either of two directions traditionally believed to be unlucky: a direction contrary to the apparent course of the sun; and counter-clockwise. The former belief must have been inconvenient, to say the least, for dwellers on western coasts. The correct usage of the term in modern parlance is in relation to the course followed by your spouse in reversing the family car up the driveway.

WITLING *n.* A mere pretender to wit; a petty smart aleck. In response to a successful sally at your expense, you slap the offender genially on the back and exclaim: 'Ah, you're becoming quite a little witling, Nigel – we shall have to be on our guard against your little whimsicalities, shan't we?' The repetition of the word *little* helps to create the right effect.

WORD-GRUBBER *n.* One who is particular about fine points of verbal usage and who himself uses long and unusual words in everyday speech. An eighteenth-century slang term.

X

XANTHIPPE *n.* A shrewish, peevish, bad-tempered wife. From the name of Socrates' wife, said to have been such a one. Whilst at first it may seem surprising that the wise and good Socrates, of all people, should have had such a person as helpmeet, on reflection it seems less so. Imagine the effect on an initially happy and well-balanced young woman of being subjected daily to the Socratic Method – of having every detail of her housekeeping, her *oniomania* (q.v.), her personal behavior, etc., subjected to calm, friendly, benevolent, and relentlessly logical cross-examination. Perhaps the above word ought to be used instead to describe a wife who has to put up with a dry-as-dust egghead of a husband who never does anything she asks him to without first requesting that she define her terms and enumerate her alternatives.

XANTHODONTOUS *a.* Having yellow teeth. Included here only because of its interest to abecedarians, being the only remotely deprecatory adjective known to the author that begins with *x*. (See *abecedarian insult, an.*)

XENOGENESIS *n.* The fancied progeniture of a living organism completely different from either of its parents. A term invented by imaginative scientists of an earlier era for something that modern science declares to be impossible. Still, there is always hope. When the gruesome Brett and Samantha break to you the news of their engagement, you either congratulate them in terms of their mutual compatibility or console them in terms of their looking forward to the possibility of xenogenesis – your choice of remark depending upon whether you wish to be ostracized by them after the wedding reception, or immediately. A further ploy would be to console them by referring to the possibility of parthenogenesis, which is reproduction without sexual union.

XENOMANIA *n.* An obsessive mania for foreign customs, traditions, manners, institutions, fashions, etc. Nowadays this is called multiculturalism.

XENOPUS *n.* An African toad with teeth in its upper jaw, tentacles on the side of its head, webbed hind feet, and claws on its toes. Now don't say you didn't learn anything new from this book.

XYLOPHAGE *n.* An insect that eats wood. 'Do you have much trouble with xylophages in your hair?' might be a somewhat unsubtle Insult Concealed for use by a young *whippersnapper* (q.v.) against his elder sister, in retaliation for her monopolization of the bathroom for the purpose of perfecting her coiffure.

Y

YANKER *n.* According to Webster, an obsolete Scottish word for which there are, or were, three separate meanings: (i) a smart stroke or blow, (ii) an agile or clever girl, and (iii) a great falsehood, or whopper. How the three meanings relate to each other is beyond the author, but he suspects that it may have something to do with the great mystery of the Scottish kilt.

YCLEPT *a.* and **YESTREEN** *n.* and *adv.* These two words mean named and yesterday evening respectively. Two more of the author's archaisms, guaranteed to exasperate friends and relatives. For maximum effect, use in close juxtaposition to a modernism. 'Yestreen, as I was enjoying a television program yclept *Star Trek*, ...'

YELLOW JACK *n.* The quarantine flag. 'Hoist the yellow jack!' you cry on first beholding the tell-tale pustules on your six-year-old's tummy.

YEMELESS *a.* Negligent. 'Well,' you say to the service-station proprietor as you pay for your grease and oil change, 'I suppose I can rely on your *younkers* [q.v.] in the service bay to have been every bit as yemeless as usual.' He nods and smiles uncomprehendingly and you go on your way with at least some sense of satisfaction in return for the emptying of your wallet.

YETHHOUNDS *n.* A pack of phantom hounds pursuing a lady. From old English folklore. *Yeth* comes from heath. Also called wishhounds. Wisely is it said that the English have a word for everything. How this particular one first came into existence is a mystery to the author, even allowing for the penchant of the English for specialist hunting dogs (see *harrier*). There appears to be no equivalent term for a pack of phantom hounds pursuing a gentleman.

YIRN *v.* To whine; to pout, or show petulance by facial grimaces. Pronounced the same as *yearn*. 'My husband is an idealist; he's always yirning for something.'

YISSE *v.* Desire, covet. On arriving at Colonel Carstairs's bridge party, you give his newly nubile daughter Amanda an *avuncular* (q.v.) pat on the head, saying to her father: 'Ah, I yisse this miss, I wis.' Knowing your penchant for childish wordplay, he chuckles politely and you head for the card table, already one trick up.

YLEM *n.* The primordial substance from which all the elements in the universe were supposed by early philosophers to have been formed. Thought by the ancients to have been water, by the moderns to be hydrogen, and by the Chinese to be monosodium glutamate.

YOUNKER *n.* Youngling, youth – more especially a male youth. Originally meaning a young gentleman, knight, or gallant, this word has gradually acquired a faintly pejorative signification, and now has connotations of callowness, inexperience, and even thick-headedness. (See *yemeless*.)

Z

ZAFTIG *a.* Desirably plump and curvaceous. Suitable for the Compliment Concealed. 'Ah, zaftig, très zaftig,' you murmur when your employer's wife enters the room.

ZOANTHROPY *n.* A pathological conviction on the part of a human that he or she is an animal – or, more correctly, a nonhuman animal. 'Is Simon's zoanthropy improving at all, now that he's a sophomore?'

ZORI *n.* (pl.) The Superior Person's word for thongs, that peculiarly aestival form of footwear commonly employed for the purpose of jamming the wearer's foot underneath brake pedals, tripping him up in public places and upon acutely serrated seaside rockformations, and rendering the sound of his coming and going akin to that of a flock of migrating ducks.

ZUGZWANG *n.* A state of play in a game of chess such that any of the various moves open to the player with the next move will damage his position. He is then said to be 'in zugzwang.' The term has obvious potential as a descriptive of certain stock situations of married life:

· Husband notices that floor is littered with assorted debris. If he (a) picks it all up, wife accuses him of regarding her as slovenly; if he (b) leaves it where it is, wife accuses him of never doing anything to help her around the house; if he (c) picks half of it up, wife accuses him of laziness. He is thus 'in zugzwang.'

· Wife notices gas gauge is on empty when husband is trying to start car. If she (a) asks him whether car has run out of gas, he will angrily tell her to shut up while he tries to listen to the motor; if she (b) says nothing, it will take him ten minutes to discover the cause of the trouble; if she (c) simply tells him that gas tank is empty, he will undergo severe loss of face and take it out on her for the rest of the evening. She is thus 'in zugzwang.'

ZZXJOANW *n.* A Maori drum. The recommended use is in Scrabble. The technique is to save up, at all costs, the letters *Z, X, J, O,* and *W* (or a blank that can be used in place of any you don't manage to acquire); to wait for a dangling *AN* on which you can build; and then to strike. The satisfaction to be derived from this single act altogether outweighs whatever chagrin you might otherwise experience through losing the game, as you assuredly will – even that experienced through losing six games in succession, if need be, before you can effect your coup.